Lonely Planet

KT-444-016

Pocket
VENICE

TOP SIGHTS • LOCAL LIFE • MADE EASY

Alison Bing

In This Book

QuickStart Guide

Your keys to understanding the city – we help you decide what to do and how to do it

Need to Know
Tips for a smooth trip

Neighbourhoods
What's where

Explore Venice

The best things to see and do, by Neighbourhood

Top Sights
Make the most of your visit

Local Life
The insider's city

The Best of Venice

The city's highlights in handy lists to help you plan

Best Walks
See the city on foot

Venice's Best...
The best experiences

Survival Guide

Tips and tricks for a seamless, hassle-free city experience

Getting Around
Travel like a local

Essential Information
Including where to stay

Our selection of the city's best places to eat, drink and experience:

◉ **Sights**

✖ **Eating**

🍷 **Drinking**

✩ **Entertainment**

🔒 **Shopping**

These symbols give you the vital information for each listing:

📞 Telephone Numbers	👪 Family-Friendly
🕐 Opening Hours	🐾 Pet-Friendly
🅿 Parking	🚌 Bus
🚭 Nonsmoking	⛴ Ferry
@ Internet Access	Ⓜ Metro
📶 Wi-Fi Access	Ⓢ Subway
🥗 Vegetarian Selection	🚋 Tram
🍴 English-Language Menu	🚆 Train

Find each listing quickly on maps for each neighbourhood:

Bar Hemingway

16 🍷 Map p233, B2

Legend has it that Hemi
self, wielding a machine
rate this timber-pan
ered bar during
showpiece is a
en by Papa ar
town. Dress
s.com; Hôtel Rit
; 🕐6.30pm-2a

Lonely Planet's Venice

Lonely Planet Pocket Guides are designed to get you straight to the heart of the city.

Inside you'll find all the must-see sights, plus tips to make your visit to each one really memorable. We've split the city into easy-to-navigate s and provided clear maps so you'll find your way around with ease. Our expert authors have searched out the best of the city: walks, food, nightlife and shopping, to name a few. Because you want to explore, our 'Local Life' pages will take you to some of the most exciting areas to experience the real .

And of course you'll find all the practical tips you need for a smooth trip: itineraries for short visits, how to get around, and how much to tip the guy who serves you a drink at the end of a long day's exploration.

It's your guarantee of a really great experience.

Our Promise

You can trust our travel infor-mation because Lonely Planet authors visit the places we write about, each and every edition. We never accept freebies for positive coverage, so you can rely on us to tell it like it is.

QuickStart Guide **7**

Explore Venice **21**

The Best of Venice 137

Venice's Best Walks

Venice's' Best ...

Survival Guide 161

QuickStart Guide

Welcome to Venice

'Ooooooeeeee!' Gondoliers call out in narrow canals. With the world's highest density of Unesco-protected masterpieces, Venice will earn gasps from you too. Once you've seen palaces built on water, partied like Casanova in costume and eaten chorus lines of red-footed lagoon scallops, you'll greet every canal bend with anticipation.

Gondolas, Bacino di San Marco
KEN WELSH / GETTY IMAGES ©

Venice
Top Sights

Basilica di San Marco (p24)

Once you step inside these Gothic portals, the crowd hushes to a collective sigh. Glittering mosaics cover the basilica's domes with heavenly visions of hovering angels and skipping saints – a uniquely uplifting experience.

JURGAR / GETTY IMAGES ©

I Frari (p70)

No one lights up a room quite like Titian's red-hot Madonna at I Frari. Even in a vast Gothic cathedral lined with serene masterpieces and sombre tombs, you can almost warm your hands from her radiant glow.

Rialto Market (p72)

Supermarket specimens can't compare to glistening lagoon seafood at the Rialto Market, where one culinary secret has been kept in the open for 600 years: food tastes better when it's fresh, seasonal and local.

Gallerie dell'Accademia (p50)

They've been censored and stolen, raised eyebrows and inspired generosity: all the fuss over Venetian paintings becomes understandable here. Prepare for colour, drama and baroque portraits you'll swear are winking at you.

Chiesa di San Giorgio Maggiore (p120)

Blinking is natural when faced with Palladio's strikingly classical, white Istrian stone church, and its shimmering reflection in blue lagoon waters. But look further: you'll find Tintorettos and contemporary art lurking in its shadows.

Scuola Grande di San Rocco (p68)

During Venice's darkest days, flashes of genius appeared: Tintoretto's loaded paintbrush streaked across the Scuola Grande di San Rocco's ceilings like a lightning bolt, offering glimmers of hope in the long shadow of the plague.

Palazzo Ducale (p28)

Other cities have grim government offices; Venice has the Palazzo Ducale, a lacy pink Gothic palace lined with Renaissance masterpieces to impress visiting dignitaries (that's you). After 600 years, it still works like a charm.

Peggy Guggenheim Collection (p52)

She dodged Nazis, collected lovers and spent a fortune supporting avant-garde artists: Peggy Guggenheim broadened the world's horizons with her palatial showcase of Kandinskys, Calders, Rothkos and other breakthrough modernists.

Campo del Ghetto Nuovo & the Ghetto (p92)

Explore the tiny island that offered refuge from the Inquisition, bailed out the Venetian empire and sparked a Renaissance in thought: the Ghetto, historical home of Venice's Jewish community.

Basilica di Santa Maria Assunta & Torcello (p122)

Once your eyes adjust to the floating Gothic splendour of Venice, Torcello alters your entire outlook. This island wilderness was once a Byzantine trading empire, and the basilica's golden mosaics prove it.

Venice Local Life

Insider tips to help you find the real city

To get to know Venice from the inside out, hit the *calli* (alleys) to find artisans' studios, music venues and *bacari* (hole-in-the-wall bars) for glimpses of Venetian life after hours and behind the scenes, and then visit the outer islands Venetians have called home for a millennium.

Music in San Marco (p32)

▶ Opera
▶ Baroque music

No other city provides a soundtrack quite like Venice: divas tickle Tintoretto-frescoed ceilings with glory notes; Vivaldi reverberates through churches purpose-built for baroque acoustics; and violins play toe-tapping tarantella over coffee in Piazza San Marco.

Happy Hour in Campo Santa Margherita (p54)

▶ Spritz cocktails
▶ Local wines

Venetian dialect isn't easy – but after a *giro d'ormbra* (happy hour) in Campo Santa Margherita, it trips right off the tongue. Start with a *spritz* (*prosecco* and bitters cocktail), advance to topnotch wines and make room for new friends at the bar with a hearty *Benvegnù!* (Welcome!)

Fashion Finds (p74)

▶ Artisan accessories
▶ Venetian fashions

Venice's signature style is no accident – it's the result of artisan traditions refined through centuries, design innovation borrowed from Biennales and fearless creativity forged in Murano furnaces. Head straight to Venice's style sources, and make your own Venetian fashion statement.

Cicheti Circuit (p94)

▶ Creative seafood
▶ Venetian small plates

While desperate daytrippers resort to reheated pizza slices in San Marco, savvy gourmands hit bar counters across Cannaregio by 6:30pm for prime *cicheti* (Venetian tapas): scampi with grilled artichokes, plump *polpette* (meatballs) and wild-leek *bacala mantecato* (creamy cod).

Murano Art Glass (p124)

▶ Art glass showrooms
▶ Glass museum pieces

Fiery passions and delicate handling are essential in love – and in Murano's legendary *fornaci* (furnaces), where master

Burano (p132)

artisans have blown glass for 600 years. Learn trade secrets at Museo del Vetro, and score museum-quality mementos in Murano's studio-showrooms.

Getting Creative in Giudecca (p126)

▶ Art venues
▶ Creative cuisine

Venice captured the world's imagination with red-hot paintings, baroque music and the first film festival – but you don't need to wait for the next Biennale to glimpse ahead of the creative curve. Giudecca

is putting theatre in arsenals, pioneering prison cuisine, and channelling tidal rhythms with canalside jazz.

Lido Bars & Beaches (p128)

▶ Beaches
▶ Al fresco entertainment

Swanky Liberty villas rise majestically behind circus-striped beach cabanas along Venice's sandy beachfront. Beach umbrellas pop up in May through September along with open-air dining, and leisurely happy hours stretch into nighttime beach clubbing.

Other prime spots to experience Venice like a local:

Gallery-hop San Marco (p37)

Squero San Trovaso (p60)

Showtime at the Scuola (p63)

Tea in a Lagoon of Espresso (p85)

Dalla Marisa (p101)

Veneto Wine-Tasting (p103)

Wagnerian drama at the Casino (p105)

Colourful Burano (p132)

Boating on the Lagoon (p135)

Venice
Day Planner

Day One

If you have just one day in Venice, make it stellar. Start your day with cappuccino accompanied by violins at **Caffe Florian** (p33), then go for maximum mosaic dazzle at **Basilica di San Marco** (p24). Drift through constellations of contemporary art stars at **Palazzo Grassi** (p36), then discover where Bohemian chic was invented at **Museo Fortuny** (p36).

Follow your rumbling stomach across Ponte di Rialto (Rialto Bridge) to **All'Arco** (p80) for Francesco and Matteo's five-star *cicheti* (Venetian tapas) creations. See where top chefs get their Michelin-starred ideas at **Rialto Market** (p72), and where artists and designers find inspiration at **Fondazione Prada** (p78). Slip into something less comfortable: the costume collection at **Palazzo Mocenigo** (p79), where stiff baroque undergarments underpin major costume drama. Gloat over your own **fashion finds** (p74) with toasts at **Al Prosecco** (p83).

Starlight helps you navigate the maze of the former red-light district near Ponte delle Tette to dinner at **Antiche Carampane** (p80); or grab a bite at **Al Pesador** (p81) to make it in time for the night's all-star performance at **La Fenice** (p43).

Day Two

Your second day in Venice is packed with international intrigue. Begin the day in prison on the **Itinerari Segreti** (p31) (Secret Passages) tour of **Palazzo Ducale** (p28), and plot your escape to browse recycled-banner totes made by Venice prison collective **Malefatte** (p45) before a lavish lunch at **A Beccafico** (p38).

Napoleon warehoused masterpieces looted from churches across Northern Italy in a Palladio-designed convent – but when he left, the collection remained in the **Accademia** (p50). Spend an afternoon here, and you'll concede the emperor had excellent taste in stolen Venetian paintings. For quality time with modern masterpieces, head around to the palatial home of Jewish American collector **Peggy Guggenheim** (p52). Afterwards, head to happy hour in Campo **Santa Margherita** (p54).

Savour the lagoon-seafood pasta and international wine menu at **Enoteca Ai Artisti** (p60), then hear Vivaldi played as a fitting soundtrack for this city of intrigue by **Interpreti Veneziani** (p33). End the night gliding down the shimmering Grand Canal on a *vaporetto* (passenger ferry) or gondola, and plot your return visit to Venice.

Short on time?
We've arranged Venice's must-sees into these day-by-day itineraries to make sure you see the very best of the city in the time you have available.

Day Three

Find heaven on earth on your third day in Venice. Skies are always Tiepolo blue inside baroque **Ca' Rezzonico** (p58), while lightning strikes inside Tintoretto's stormy canvases at nearby **Scuola Grande di San Rocco** (p68). At **I Frari** (p71), bask in the glow of the flushed Madonna, ascending to glory in Titian-red robes.

Pizza in a sunny *campo* (piazza) is a slice of heaven at **Birraria La Corte** (p82). Next, hop the vaporetto to **Ca' d'Oro** (p98) for Renaissance altarpieces and Grand Canal views framed by Venetian Gothic splendour. Stop for cloudlike hazelnut gelato at **Gelateria Ca' d'Oro** (p101) before your tour of Ghetto synagogues begins at **Museo Ebraico** (p93).

Sublime *cicheti* and DOC wines await at **Al Timon** (p95), before heading across the Grand Canal for chamber-music concerts under rosy, Sebastiano Ricci cherub ceilings at **Palazetto Bru Zane** (p85). For a diabolically decadent twist, end the night with a glass of Amarone and snacks at **I Rusteghi** (p41).

Day Four

Island-hop the day away, beginning with Byzantine splendour in Torcello's **Basilica di Santa Maria Assunta** (p122). Head to the colourful island fishing village of **Burano** (p132) for photo-ops and lagoon seafood lunch in the Venissa vineyard.

Hit Murano glass showcases – gently – to score museum-quality tableware. Take the *vaporetto* from Murano to San Zaccaria, where you'll catch another *vaporetto* to reach Palladio's **Chiesa di San Giorgio Maggiore** (p120) as the afternoon sun turns it pure gold. Check out the Tintorettos by the altar, then nip around back to see contemporary art at **Fondazione Giorgio Cini** (p121).

Hop one *vaporetto* stop to Giudecca for dinner canalside at **I Figli delle Stelle** (p127), with stirring views of San Marco and occasional weekend jazz shows. From May through September, take the *vaporetto* to the Lido for Venice Film Festival premieres, free concerts and DJ sets on the beach.

Need to Know

**For more information,
see Survival Guide (p161)**

Currency
Euro (€)

Language
Italian, with some Venet (Venetian dialect)

Visas
Not required by EU nationals. Nationals of Australia, Brazil, Canada, Japan, New Zealand and the USA do not need visas for visits up to 90 days.

Money
ATMs are widely available.

Mobile Phones
GSM and tri-band phones can be used in Italy with a local SIM card, including most European and Australian phones. Other phones should be set to roaming.

Time
GMT/UTC plus one hour during winter; GMT/UTC plus two hours during summer daylight saving

Plugs & Adaptors
Most plugs have two or three round pins. The current is 220V to 230V, 50Hz.

Tipping
Optional 10% for good service at restaurants where not included in the bill; optional for water taxis and hotel porters; leave spare change for prompt service at bar and cafe counters.

❶ Before You Go

Your Daily Budget

Budget less than €120
▸ Dorm bed: €22–€30
▸ *Cicheti* (Venetian tapas): €5–€15
▸ *Traghetto* ride: €0.50

Midrange €120–€250
▸ B&B: €50–€150
▸ 12-hour *vaporetto* ticket: €18
▸ Midrange dinner: €25–€45

Top End more than €250
▸ Boutique hotel: €150-plus
▸ Gondola ride: €80
▸ Top-end dinner: €45–€60

Useful Websites

▸ **Lonely Planet** (www.lonelyplanet.com/italy/venice) Expert travel advice.

▸ **Venice Comune** (www.comune.venezia.it) City of Venice site; high-water alerts.

▸ **Venezia da Vivere** (www.veneziadavivere.com) Music performances, art, nightlife.

Advance Planning

Two months before Book accommodation for high season; buy tickets to La Fenice operas, Venice Film Festival premieres and Biennale openings.

Three weeks before Check special-event calendars at www.aguestinvenice.com and www.veneziadavivere.com; reserve lagoon boat day trips.

One week before Make restaurant reservations; book tickets to major attractions and events online at www.venetoinside.com or www.veniceconnected.com.

❷ Arriving in Venice

Most visitors enter Venice by plane at Marco Polo Airport (VCE) or by train at Stazione Santa Lucia (Venezia-SL). Marco Polo Airport is on the mainland, with connections to Venice via bus (www.atvo.it; www.actv.it), reliable passenger ferry (www.alilaguna.it) and water taxi. Stazione Santa Lucia (also called Ferrovia) is situated within Venice, and several *vaporetto* lines depart from docks in front of the station.

✈ From Marco Polo Airport

Destination	Best Transport
Piazzale Roma	ATVO bus
San Marco	Alilaguna ferry Linea Blu (Blue Line)
Rialto	Alilaguna ferry Linea Arancia (Orange Line)
Dorsoduro	Alilaguna ferry Linea Blu
Stazione Santa Lucia	Alilaguna ferry Linea Arancia
Lido	Alilaguna ferry Linea Blu

From Stazione Santa Lucia (Ferrovia)

Destination	Best Transport
Piazzale Roma	walking via Ponte di Calatrava
Rialto	*Vaporetto* lines 1, 2 & N
San Marco	*Vaporetto* lines 1 & N
Dorsoduro	*Vaporetto* lines 1 & N
Fondamenta Nuove (Cannaregio)	*Vaporetto* lines 41 & 42
Lido	*Vaporetto* lines 1 & N

❸ Getting Around

Walking is the most scenic and often easiest way to navigate Venice – and it's free. The other way to navigate this city on the water is by boat, and there are plenty of boating options. Cars and bicycles can be used on the Lido.

🚤 Vaporetto

Passenger ferries run throughout Venice and to outlying islands – note the line and direction at the dock to make sure you catch the right boat. Single rides cost €7; for frequent use, get a timed pass (24-hour passes cost €20). Limited wheelchair access.

Gondola

Not mere transport but an adventure – and the best way to slip into Venice's smaller canals and glimpse the city behind the scenes. Count on €80 per 40 minutes plus tip, and surcharges after dark. Music costs extra.

Water Taxis

The only door-to-door option, but fares are steep at €8.90 plus €1.80 per minute, plus surcharges for nighttime, luggage, large group and hotel services. Book ahead.

Traghetto

Locals use this daytime public gondola service (€0.50) to cross the Grand Canal between bridges.

🚲 Bicycle

Only allowed on the Lido, where bike hire is available and affordable (from €10).

🚗 Car

No cars are allowed in Venice beyond Piazzale Roma, where parking starts at €24 per day. Cars can be used on the Lido.

Venice
Neighbourhoods

San Polo & Santa Croce (p66)

Treasure hunts in these side-by-side *sestieri* uncover priceless Titians, courtesan couture, scientific wonders and culinary gems.

👁 Top Sights

Scuola Grande di San Rocco

I Frari

Rialto Market

Campo del Ghetto Nuovo & the Ghetto

Rialto Market

Scuola Grande di San Rocco

I Frari

Peggy Guggenheim Collection

Gallerie dell'Accademia

Dorsoduro & the Accademia (p48)

Venice's historic artists' quarter is packed with censored paintings, life-saving architecture and marathon happy hours.

👁 Top Sights

Gallerie dell'Accademia

Peggy Guggenheim Collection

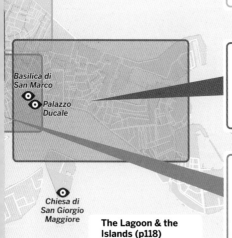

Cannaregio & the Ghetto (p90)

Follow serene canalbanks for bargain *cicheti* (Venetian tapas), priceless Tintorettos and a tiny island with a big history.

⊙ Top Sights

Campo del Ghetto Nuovo & the Ghetto

Castello (p106)

Between Arsenale shipyards and Biennale pavilions, you can dine like a doge, drink like a sailor and find the inner calm of a Greek icon.

San Marco & Palazzo Ducale (p22)

A downtown like no other: gondola traffic, acres of golden mosaics and legendary escapes from a pink Gothic prison.

⊙ Top Sights

Basilica di San Marco

Palazzo Ducale

Basilica di San Marco

Palazzo Ducale

Chiesa di San Giorgio Maggiore

The Lagoon & the Islands (p118)

⊙ Top Sights

Chiesa di San Giorgio Maggiore

Basilica di Santa Maria Assunta & Torcello

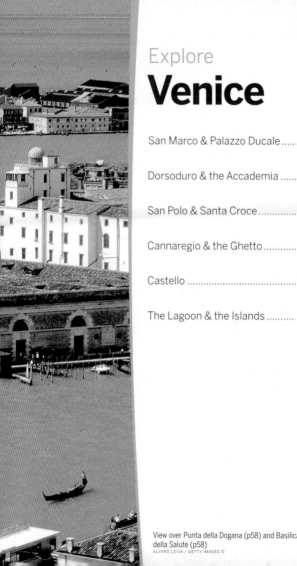

Explore
Venice

View over Punta della Dogana (p58) and Basilica di Santa Maria della Salute (p58)
ALVARO LEIVA / GETTY IMAGES ©

Explore

San Marco & Palazzo Ducale

So many world-class attractions are packed into San Marco that some visitors never leave – and others are reluctant to visit, fearing crowds. But why deny yourself the pleasures of La Fenice, Basilica di San Marco, Palazzo Ducale and Museo Correr? Judge for yourself whether they earn their reputations – but don't stop there. The back-streets are packed with galleries, boutiques and *enoteche* (wine bars).

The Sights in a Day

☀ Join the chorus of gasps from the crowd as you enter the **Basilica di San Marco** (p24) to discover glittering angels dancing across golden mosaic domes. Explore Venice's darkest secrets in the **Palazzo Ducale** (p28) attic prison on the Itinerari Segreti tour, then jail-break for lavish, sunny lunches at **A Beccafico** (p38).

☀ Hit the backstreets between Piazza San Marco and the Rialto to find Venetian artisans handcrafting handbags, travel journals and glass jewellery. Hidden in the shadows of historic Santa Maria del Giglio and La Fenice theatre are Venice's best contemporary art galleries, supplying steady inspiration between Biennales. Detour for history-making fashion and modern art at **Museo Fortuny** (p36), but arrive at San Marco *bacari* (bars) by 6.30pm for first dibs on *cicheti* (Venetian tapas).

☾ Savour sunset cocktails at **Harry's Bar** (p41), but don't miss the overture at **La Fenice** (p43). Return to moonlit Piazza San Marco for a tango across the square, and watch the Moors strike midnight atop **Torre dell'Orologio** (p36), heralding another day in the life of San Marco's charmed existence.

For a local's day in San Marco, see p32.

◎ Top Sights

○ Local Life

♥ Best of Venice

Best Museums

Best Architecture

Getting There

🚤 **Vaporetto** Lines 1 and N along the Grand Canal; Line 2 stops near San Marco at San Zaccaria.

Walking Follow yellow-signed shortcuts from Rialto through shop-lined Marzarie to Piazza San Marco.

Top Sights
Basilica di San Marco

Creating Venice's architectural wonder took nearly 800 years and one saintly barrel of lard. In AD 828, wily Venetian merchants allegedly smuggled St Mark's corpse out of Egypt in a barrel of pork fat to avoid inspection by Muslim customs authorities. Venice built a golden basilica around its stolen saint, whose bones were misplaced twice during construction.

St Mark's Basilica

◉ Map p34, H3

www.basilicasanmarco.it

Piazza San Marco

admission free

🕑9.45am-5pm Mon-Sat, 2-5pm Sun, to 4pm winter

🚤San Marco

Domes of Basilica di San Marco

Don't Miss

Portals

Venice created the official doge's chapel in its own cosmopolitan image, with Byzantine onion-bulb domes, Greek cross layout and marble cladding from Syria, Egypt and Palestine – priceless trophies from Crusades conquests and battles with Genoa. The basilica's facade ripples and crests like a wave, its five niched portals capped with shimmering mosaics and frothy stonework arches.

In the far-left portal, lunette mosaics dating from 1270 show St Mark's stolen body arriving at the basilica – a story reprised in 1660 lunette mosaics on the second portal from the right. Grand entrances are made through the central portal, under an ornate triple arch with Egyptian purple porphyry columns and 13th- to 14th-century reliefs of vines, virtues and astrological signs.

Dome Mosaics

Blinking is natural upon your first glimpse of the basilica's glittering mosaics, many made with 24-carat gold leaf fused onto the back of the glass to represent divine light. Just inside the narthex (vestibule) glitter the basilica's oldest mosaics: *Apostles with the Madonna*, standing sentry by the main door for more than 950 years.

The atrium's medieval **Dome of Genesis** depicts the separation of sky and water with surprisingly abstract motifs, anticipating modern art by 650 years. Last Judgment mosaics cover the atrium vault and the Apocalypse looms large in vault mosaics over the gallery.

Mystical transfusions occur in the **Dome of the Holy Spirit**, where a dove's blood streams onto the heads of saints. In the central, 13th-century **Cupola of the Ascension**, angels swirl overhead while dreamy-eyed St Mark rests on the

☑ **Top Tips**

▶ Queues rarely exceed 15-minutes wait. Book 'Skip the Line' access online April to October (www.venetoinside.com; €1 booking fee).

▶ Pala d'Oro offers doge's-eye views of the basilica.

▶ Dress respectfully (ie knees and shoulders covered) and leave large bags around the corner at free one-hour baggage storage.

▶ Free guided tours explain mosaic theological messages (11am Monday to Saturday, April to October, by reservation).

✕ **Take a Break**

Don't settle for sad pizza from nearby kiosks; pasta and *cicheti* at Cavatappi (p40) are a three-minute walk away. Caffè Lavena (p32) offers Piazza San Marco's best deal: €1 for espresso at the bar.

pendentive. Scenes from St Mark's life unfold over the main altar, in vaults flanking the **Dome of the Prophets** (best seen from the Pala d'Oro).

Pala d'Oro

Tucked behind the main altar containing **St Mark's sarcophagus** is the Pala d'Oro, studded with 2000 emeralds, amethysts, sapphires, rubies, pearls and other gemstones. But the most priceless treasures here are biblical figures in vibrant cloisonné, begun in Constantinople in AD 976 and finished by Venetian goldsmiths in 1209.

The enamelled saints have wild, unkempt beards and wide eyes fixed on Jesus, who glances sideways at a studious St Mark as Mary throws up her hands in wonder – an understandable reaction to such a captivating scene. Look closely to spot touches of Venetian whimsy: falcon-hunting scenes in medallions along the bottom, and the by-now-familiar scene of St Mark's body smuggled out of Egypt on the right.

Tesoro

Holy bones and booty from the Crusades fill the treasury, including a 10th-century rock-crystal ewer with winged feet made for Fatimid Caliph al-'Aziz-bi-llah. Don't miss bejeweled 12th-century Archangel Michael, featuring tiny, feisty enamelled saints that appear ready to break free of

Basilica di San Marco

Ground Floor

their golden setting and mount a miniature attack on evil. Velvet-padded boxes preserve doges' remains alongside alleged saints' relics, including St Roch's femur, St Mark's thumb, the arm St George used to slay the dragon and even a lock of the Madonna's hair.

Museo

San Marco remained the doge's chapel until 1807, and the ducal treasures upstairs in the museum put a king's ransom to shame. Gilt bronze horses taken by Venice from Constantinople were stolen in turn by Napoleon, but eventually returned to the basilica and installed in the first-floor gallery. Portals lead from the gallery to giddiness-inducing **Loggia dei Cavalli**, where reproductions of the horses gallop off the balcony over Piazza San Marco.

In the Museo's restored 13th- to 16th-century mosaic fragments, the Prophet Abraham is all ears and raised eyebrows, as though scandalised by Venetian gossip. On an interior balcony, Salviati's restored 1542–52 mosaic of the Virgin's family tree shows Mary's ancestors perched on branches, alternately chatting and ignoring one another, as families do. Hidden over the side altar is the **doge's banquet hall**, where dignitaries wined and dined among lithe stucco figures of Music, Poetry and Peace.

NICO DE PASQUALE PHOTOGRAPHY / GETTY IMAGES ©

Interior, Basilica di San Marco

Exterior

The brick basilica is clad in patchworks of marbles and reliefs from Syria, Egypt and Palestine – priceless trophies from Crusades conquests and battles with Genoa. At the southwestern corner is the Four Tetrarchs, an Egyptian porphyry statue supposedly representing four emperors of ancient Rome looted from Constantinople.

Top Sights
Palazzo Ducale

Don't be fooled by the genteel Gothic elegance: under its lacy pink facade and rosy Veronese ceilings, the Ducal Palace flexes serious political muscle. The seat of Venice's government for nearly seven centuries, this powerhouse stood the test of fires, storms and conspiracies – only to be outwitted by Casanova, the notorious seducer, who escaped from the attic prison.

Map p34, H4

848 08 20 00

palazzoducale.visitmuve.it

Piazzetta San Marco 52

adult/reduced €16/8

8.30am-7pm Apr-Oct, to 5.30pm Nov-Mar

San Zaccaria

Angel carving, Palazzo Ducale

Don't Miss

Exterior

After fire gutted the original palace in 1577, Antonio da Ponte restored its Gothic grandeur. The white Istrian stone and Veronese pink marble palace caps a graceful colonnade with medieval capitals depicting key Venetian guilds.

The pretty arcaded **loggia** along the *piazzetta* (little square) served a solemn purpose: death sentences were read between the ninth and 10th columns from the left.

First Floor

Climb the **Scala dei Censori** (Censors' Stairs) to the **Doge's Apartments**, where the doge lived under 24-hour guard with a short commute to work up a secret staircase. Walk up a couple of steps and turn around to spot Titian's *St Christopher* wading across troubled lagoon waters over the archway.

The **Sala del Scudo** (Shield Room) is covered with world maps that reveal the extents of Venetian power (and the limits of its cartographers) between c 1483 and 1762.

Sala delle Quattro Porte

Head up Sansovino's 24-carat gilt stuccowork **Scala d'Oro** (Golden Staircase). In Palladio-designed Sala delle Quattro Porte (Hall of the Four Doors), ambassadors awaited ducal audiences under a lavish display of Venice's virtues by Giovanni Cambi. Other convincing shows of Venetian superiority include Titian's 1576 *Doge Antonio Grimani Kneeling Before Faith* and Tiepolo's 1740s *Venice Receiving Gifts of the Sea from Neptune*.

☑ Top Tips

▶ On the east side of the courtyard arcade were the dreaded Poggi (Wells), where prisoners shivered below water level – now a baggage deposit is installed in their place.

▶ Photography is not allowed indoors, but the excellent Palazzo Ducale bookshop has postcards and art books covering major artworks.

▶ Admission also covers entry to Museo Correr (p36) or you can use the Museum Pass (p166).

✕ Take a Break

The combined ticket and Museum Pass include Museo Correr, where Caffè delle Arte offers *panini* (sandwiches) with views of Basilica di San Marco. Local legend claims that after his Palazzo Ducale prison escape, Casanova stopped by Caffè Florian (p33) for a drink – why not follow suit?

Doge's Palace

Second Floor

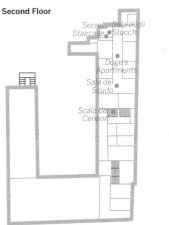

First Floor

Anticollegio

Delegations waited in the **Anticollegio** (Council Antechamber), where Domenico Tintoretto drew parallels between Roman gods and Venetian government: *Mercury and the Three Graces* reward Venice's industriousness with beauty, and *Minerva Dismissing Mars* is a Venetian triumph of savvy over brute force. The recently restored ceiling is Veronese's 1577 *Venice Distributing Honours,* while on the walls is Veronese's *Rape of Europe.*

Collegio & Sala del Senato

Few were granted audiences in the Palladio-designed **Collegio** (Council Room), where Veronese's 1575–78 *Virtues of the Republic* ceiling shows Venice as a blonde waving her sceptre over Justice and Peace. Father-son team Jacopo and Domenico Tintoretto show Venice keeping company with Apollo, Mars and Mercury in their *Triumph of Venice* ceiling for the **Sala del Senato** (Senate Hall).

Sala Consiglio dei Dieci & Sala della Bussola

Government cover-ups were never so appealing as in the Sala Consiglio dei Dieci (Trial Chambers of the Council of 10; Room 20), where Venice's star chamber plotted under Veronese's *Juno Bestowing Her Gifts on Venice.* Over the slot where anonymous treason accusations were slipped in the *Sala della Bussola* (Compass Room; Room 21) is his *St Mark in Glory* ceiling.

Sala del Maggior Consiglio

The 1419 Sala del Maggior Consiglio (Grand Council Hall) features the doge's throne against Tintoretto's politically correct *Paradise;* heaven is apparently crammed with 500 prominent Venetians, including Tintoretto patrons. Veronese's *Apotheosis of Venice* ceiling has gods and foreign dignitaries marvelling at Venice's coronation by angels. The wall frieze depicts Venice's first 76 doges; the black space is for Doge Marin Falier, who lost his head for treason in 1355.

Prisons

Sala del Magistrato alle Leggi (Hall of the Legal Magistrate) features ominous scenes by Hieronymus Bosch. Follow the path of condemned prisoners across **Ponte dei Sospiri** (Bridge of Sighs) to 16th-century **Priggione Nove** (New Prisons). Cells are graffitied with protestations of innocence and paved with marble stolen during the sacking of Constantinople.

Itinerari Segreti

Itinerari Segreti (Secret Passages; ☎041 4273 0892; adult/reduced €20/14; ⊙tours in English 9.55am, 10.45am & 11.35am, in Italian 9.30am & 11.10am, in French 10.20am & noon) is a 75-minute tour of the Piombi (Leads) prison cells and other top-secret attic rooms. See the **headquarters of the Council of Ten**, Venice's CIA; the **Chancellery**, filled with top-secret files; the **Interrogation Room**; and the cells where Casanova made his escape through the roof.

Local Life
Music in San Marco

Once Venice's dominion over the high seas ended, it discovered the power of high Cs, hiring as San Marco choirmaster Claudio Monteverdi, the father of modern opera, and bringing on baroque with Antonio Vivaldi. Today, MP3s still can't compare to Venice's live-music offerings. While Teatro La Fenice is the obvious draw for opera lovers, try these other music destinations to immerse yourself in a Venetian soundtrack.

❶ Tarantella at Caffè Lavena

Opera composer Richard Wagner had the right idea: when Venice leaves you weak in the knees, get a pick-me-up at **Lavena** (☎041 522 40 70; www.lavena .it; Piazza San Marco 133/4; drinks €1-12; ☺9.30am-11pm; 🚦San Marco). The €1 espresso at Lavena's mirrored bar is a baroque bargain – never mind the politically incorrect antique 'Moor's head' chandeliers. Spring for piazza seating to savour *caffè corretto* (coffee

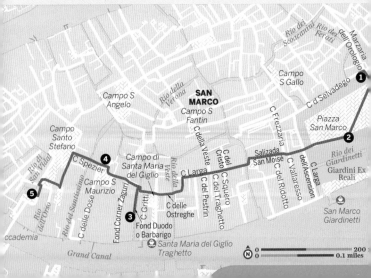

'corrected' with liquor) accompanied by Lavena's nimble violinists.

2 Tango at Caffè Florian
Florian (☏041 520 56 41; www.caffeflorian.com; Piazza San Marco 56/59; drinks €6.50-16; ⏱10am-midnight Thu-Tue; 🛋San Marco) maintains rituals established c 1720: white-jacketed waiters serve cappuccino on silver trays, and the orchestra strikes up a tango as sunsets illuminate San Marco's mosaics. Piazza seating during concerts costs €6 extra, but dreamy-eyed romantics hardly notice. Among Italy's first bars to welcome women and revolutionaries, Florian's radical-chic reputation persists with its art installations.

3 Arias at Musica a Palazzo
Hang onto your *prosecco:* at **Musica a Palazzo** (☏340 971 72 72; www.musicapalazzo.com; Palazzo Barbarigo-Minotto, Fondamenta Barbarigo o Duodo 2504; tickets incl beverage €60; ⏱doors open 8pm; 🛋Santa Maria del Giglio), the soprano's high notes imperil glassware. During 1½ hours of selected arias from Verdi or Rossini, the drama progresses from receiving-room overtures to parlour duets overlooking the Grand Canal, followed by second acts in the Tiepolo-ceilinged dining room and bedroom grand finales.

4 History at Museo della Musica
Housed in the restored neoclassical Chiesa di San Maurizio, **Museo della Musica** (☏041 241 18 40; http://www.interpretiveneziani.com/en/museo-della-musica.php; Campo San Maurizio 2761; admission free; ⏱10am-7pm; 🛋Santa Maria del Giglio) presents a collection of rare 17th- to 19th-century instruments, accompanied by informative panels on the life and times of Venice's Antonio Vivaldi. The museum is funded by Interpreti Veneziani.

5 Baroque Bravado at Interpreti Veneziani
Everything you've heard of Vivaldi from weddings and mobile ring tones is proved fantastically wrong by **Interpreti Veneziani** (☏041 277 05 61; www.interpretiveneziani.com; Chiesa San Vidal, Campo di San Vidal 2862; adult/reduced €25/20; ⏱doors open 8.30pm; 🛋Accademia), who play Vivaldi on 18th-century instruments as a soundtrack for living in this city of intrigue – you'll never listen to *The Four Seasons* again without hearing summer storms erupting over the lagoon, or snow-muffled footsteps hurrying over footbridges in winter's-night intrigues.

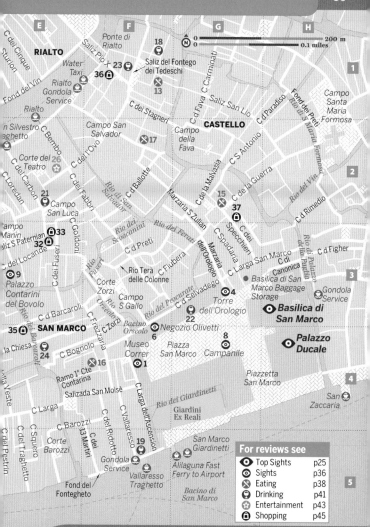

200 m
0.1 miles

RIALTO

Ponte di Rialto

Saliz Pio

Water Taxi

23

36

18

Saliz del Fontego dei Tedeschi

13

Rialto Gondola Service

C dei Stagneri

C dei Fava

C Carminati

Saliz San Lio

CASTELLO

C S Antonio

C del Paradiso

Fond dei Preti

Rio de S Maria Formosa

Campo Santa Maria Formosa

Rialto

Fond del Vin

C dei Cinque

Sturion

C dei Vin

Campo San Salvador

17

Campo della Fava

C de la Guerra

Rio del Vin

C Bembo

C dei Ovo

Corte del Teatro

26

C del Carbon

C Loredan

21

Campo San Luca

C dei Fabbri

Rio di San Salvador

C d Ballotte

Marzaria S Zullian

15

C de la Mandola

37

C de la Guerra

Rio del Rimedio

C d Rimedio

C d Figher

ampo Manin

Saliz S Paternian

32

33

C dei Fuseri

C dei Goldoni

Rio dei Scoacanini

Rio dei Ferali

C d Preti

Marzaria dell'Orologio

C Fiubera

Marzaria Spadaria

C Larga San Marco

C di Canonica

Basilica di San Marco Storage

Rio di Palazzo della Paglia

Gondola Service

9

Palazzo Contarini del Bovolo

C d Barcaroli

Rio Fuseri

Corte Zorzi

Rio Terà delle Colonne

Campo S Gallo

C d Selvadego

Rio del Procurate

4

Torre dell'Orologio

22

Basilica di San Marco Storage

Gondola Service

Basilica di San Marco

35

SAN MARCO

la Chiesa

C Barcaroli

24

C Bognolo

16

C Fiezzaria

C Zorzi

Bacino Orseolo

Negozio Olivetti

6

Museo Correr

1

Piazza San Marco

8

Campanile

Palazzo Ducale

Piazzetta San Marco

San Zaccaria

Ramo I° Cte Contarina

Salizada San Moisè

C Larga dell'Ascension

Rio del Giardinetti

Giardini Ex Reali

lla Veste

C Larga

C Barozzi

C del Ridotto

C d Martin

19

Gondola Service

Vallaresso Traghetto

Alilaguna Fast Ferry to Airport

San Marco Giardinetti

Bacino di San Marco

Corte Barozzi

Fond del Fonteghето

C del Squero

C del Traghetto

C del Pestrin

For reviews see	
◉ Top Sights	p25
◉ Sights	p36
✕ Eating	p38
🍷 Drinking	p41
★ Entertainment	p43
🔒 Shopping	p45

Sights

Museo Correr MUSEUM

 1 Map p34, F4

Napoleon lost his royal apartments over Piazza San Marco to Austrian emperor Franz Josef not long after building them, but its crowning glory remains: Jacopo Sansovino's 16th-century **Libreria Nazionale Marciana**, graced with philosophers by Veronese, Titian and Tintoretto. If you wonder how empresses sleep nights, find out in Empress' Sissi's restored, brocade-swagged suite. Afterwards, enjoy imperial views and *prosecco* (Venetian sparkling wine) in grotesque-frescoed Caffè dell'Art. (☑041 4273 0892; http://correr.visitmuve.it; Piazza San Marco 52; adult/reduced incl Palazzo Ducale €16/8 or with Museum Pass; ⊙10am-7pm Apr-Oct, to 5pm Nov-Mar; ⛴San Marco)

Palazzo Grassi MUSEUM

 2 Map p34, A4

Grand Canal gondola riders gasp at first glimpse of massive sculptures by contemporary artists like Thomas Houseago docked in front of Giorgio Masari's 1749 neoclassical palace. French billionaire François Pinault's provocative art collection overflows Palazzo Grassi, supplying Venice with sensation and scandal aplenty between Biennales – but Tadao Ando's creatively repurposed interior architecture steals the show. (☑box office 199 13 91 39, 041 523 16 80; www.palazzograssi.it; Campo San Samuele 3231; adult/reduced

€15/10, 72hr ticket incl Punta della Dogana €20/15; ⊙10am-7pm Wed-Mon; ⛴San Samuele)

Museo Fortuny MUSEUM

 3 Map p34, C3

Find design inspiration at the palatial home-studio of Art Nouveau designer Mariano Fortuny y Madrazo, whose shockingly uncorseted Delphi-goddess frocks set the standard for bohemian chic. First-floor salon walls are eclectic mood boards: Fortuny fashions and Isfahan tapestries, family portraits and James Turrell's sublime red-light installation. Look closely: Fortuny's Moorish lanterns illuminate Roberta di Camerino purses and glittering Warhols. (☑041 4273 0892; http://fortuny.visitmuve.it; Campo San Beneto 3758; adult/reduced with Museum Pass €10/8; ⊙10am-6pm Wed-Mon; ⛴Sant'Angelo)

Torre dell'Orologio LANDMARK

4 Map p34, G3

The two hardest-working men in Venice stand duty on a rooftop around the clock, and wear no pants. No need to file workers' complaints: the 'Do Mori' (Two Moors) atop Torre dell'Orologio are bronze, and their bell-hammering mechanism runs like, well, clock-work. Below, Venice's gold-leafed 15th-century timepiece tracks lunar phases. Tours climb four-storey spiral staircases past clockworks to the roof. (Clock Tower; ☑041 4273 0892; www.museicivicivenezia.it; Piazza San Marco; adult/reduced with Museum Pass €12/7; ⊙tours in

English 10am & 11am Mon-Wed, 2pm & 3pm Thu-Sun, in Italian noon & 4pm daily, in French 2pm & 3pm Mon-Wed, 10am & 11am Thu-Sun; 🚣San Marco)

Chiesa di Santa Maria del Giglio CHURCH

5 ◎ Map p34, D5

Experience awe through the ages in this compact church with a 10th-century Byzantine layout, charmingly flawed maps of Venice territories c 1678 on the facade, and three intriguing masterpieces. Veronese's *Madonna with Child* hides behind the altar, Tintoretto's four evangelists flank the organ, and Peter Paul Rubens' *Mary with St John* in the **Molin Chapel** features a characteristically chubby baby Jesus. (Santa Maria Zobenigo; www.chorusvenezia.org; Campo di Santa Maria del Giglio; admission €3 or with Chorus Pass; ◉10am-5pm Mon-Sat; 🚣Santa Maria del Giglio)

Negozio Olivetti LANDMARK

6 ◎ Map p34, F4

Like a revolver pulled from a petticoat, ultramodern Negozio Olivetti was an outright provocation when it first appeared under the frilly arcades of Piazza San Marco in 1958. High-tech pioneer Olivetti commissioned Venetian architect Carlo Scarpa to transform a narrow, dim souvenir shop into a sleek showcase for its typewriters and 'computing machines' (several 1948–54 models are displayed). (Olivetti Store; 📞041 522

Local Life
Gallery Hop San Marco

San Marco is not just a museum piece; slip into its backstreets to discover contemporary galleries.

Venice's most radical decor scheme is at **Caterina Tognon Arte Contemporanea** (Map p34, C5; 📞041 520 78 59; www.caterinatognon.com; Palazzo da Ponte, Calle delle Dose 2746; admission free; ◉10am-1pm & 3-7.30pm Tue-Sat; 🚣Santa Maria del Giglio), regularly reinvented by guest artists.

Quiet think pieces await discovery at **Galerie van der Koelen** (Map p34, D4; 📞041 520 74 15; www.galerie.vanderkoelen.de; Ramo Primo dei Calegheri 2566; admission free; ◉10am-12.30pm & 3.30-6.30pm Mon-Sat; 🚣Santa Maria del Giglio).

Jarach Gallery (Map p34, E4; 📞041 522 19 38; www.jarachgallery.com; Campo San Fantin 1997; admission free; ◉10am-1pm & 2.30-7.30pm Tue-Sat; 🚣Santa Maria del Giglio) highlights contemporary photography and video art.

Galleria Traghetto (Map p34, D4; 📞041 522 11 88; www.galleriatraghetto.it; Campo Santa Maria del Giglio 2543; admission free; ◉3-7pm Mon-Sat; 🚣Santa Maria del Giglio) shows gutsy pieces by young Italian artists.

83 87; www.negoziolivetti.it; Piazza San Marco 101, Procuratie Vecchie; adult/reduced incl audio tour €5/2.50; ◉11am-6.30pm Tue-Sun Apr-Oct, to 4.30pm Nov-Mar; 🚣San Marco)

Chiesa di
Santo Stefano
CHURCH

7 Map p34, C4

The free-standing bell tower behind it leans disconcertingly, but this brick Gothic church has stood tall since 1325. Credit for ship-shape splendour goes to Bartolomeo Bon for the marble entry portal and to Venetian shipbuilders, who constructed the vast wooden *carena di nave* (ship's keel) ceiling that resembles an upturned Noah's Ark. (www.chorusvenezia.org; Campo Santo Stefano; admission €3 or with Chorus Pass; ⌚10am-5pm Mon-Sat; ⛴Accademia)

Campanile
TOWER

8 Map p34, G4

The basilica's 99m-tall tower has been rebuilt twice since its initial construction in AD 888, and Galileo Galilei found it handy for testing his telescope in 1609. Critics called Bartolomeo Bon's 16th-century tower redesign ungainly, but when this version suddenly collapsed in 1902, Venetians rebuilt the tower as it was, brick by brick. (Bell Tower; www.basilicasanmarco.it; Piazza San Marco; admission €8; ⌚9am-9pm Jul-Sep, to 7pm Apr-Jun & Oct, 9.30am-3.45pm Nov-Mar; ⛴San Marco)

Palazzo
Contarini del Bovolo
PALACE

9 Map p34, E3

No need to wait for San Marco sunsets to inspire a snog: this romantic Renaissance 15th-century *palazzo* with an external spiral *bovolo* (snail-shell) stairwell is closed for restoration, but its shady courtyard offers stirring views and privacy. (Calle Contarini del Bovolo 4299; entry to open courtyard free; ⛴Sant'Angelo)

Eating

A Beccafico
ITALIAN €€

10 Map p34, C4

Far from clubby pubs lining Venice's alleyways, A Beccafico basks in the sunshine of Campo Santo Stefano and open Venetian admiration. Chef Adeli serves Sicily-size bowls of mussels under a bubbling, flaky crust. He defies Venice's cardinal rule never to mix lagoon seafood with cheese, serving squid-ink pasta with lemon zest and ricotta. Linger over feather-light Pieoropan Soave Classico, and leave with a surprisingly full belly – and wallet. (☏041 527 48 79; www.abeccafico.com; Campo Santo Stefano 2801; meals €25-45; ⌚noon-3pm & 7-11pm; ⛴Accademia)

Enoteca
al Volto
VENETIAN, CICHETI BAR €

11 Map p34, D2

Join the bar crowd working its way through the vast selection of wine and *cicheti,* or come early for a table outdoors (in summer). Inside the snug backroom that looks like a ship's hold, tuck into seaworthy bowls of pasta with *bottarga* (dried fish roe), steak drizzled with aged balsamic vinegar,

CHUCK PEFLEY / ALAMY ©

Circular staircase, Palazzo Contarini del Bovolo

and housemade ravioli. Cash only. (☎041 522 89 45; Calle Cavalli 4081; cicheti €2-4, meals under €25; ☉10am-3pm & 5.30-10pm Mon-Sat; ☺Rialto)

Bacaro Da Fiore

CICHETI BAR, VENETIAN €

 12 Map p34, C4

Attached to an upmarket trattoria, this *cicheti* counter wins Venetian loyalty with small plates of *baccala mantecato* (creamed cod), octopus-fennel salad, *arancini* (risotto balls) and Venetian *trippa* (tripe) to enjoy on a stool at the bar or on the streetside. Even with gorgeous DOC soave by the glass, meals cost a fraction of what you'd pay for table seating.

(☎041 523 53 10; www.dafiore.it; Calle delle Botteghe 3461; meals €10-15; ☉5.30-9pm Wed-Mon; ☺San Samuele)

Gelateria Suso

GELATO €

13 Map p34, F1

Indulge in gelato as rich as a doge, in original seasonal flavours like marscapone cream with fig sauce and walnuts. All Suso's gelati are locally made and free of artificial colours, and even the gluten-free flavours are extra creamy. A waffle cone with hazelnut and extra-dark chocolate passes as dinner. (☎348 564 65 45; Calle della Bissa 5453; gelati €2-5; ☉10am-10pm; ☺Rialto)

LOOK DIE BILDAGENTUR DER FOTOGRAFEN GMBH / ALAMY ©

Harry's Bar

Caffè Mandola

PANINI €

14 Map p34, D3

Carb-load before the opera or between museums with fresh focaccia heaped with tangy tuna and capers or lean *bresaola*, rocket and seasoned Grana Padano cheese. On cold days, get your *porchetta* (pork) and gorgonzola cheese *panini* toasted to gooey perfection. Plan your breaks before 1pm or after 3pm to snag a stool indoors (no extra charge). (☑041 523 76 24; Calle della Mandola 3630; panini €3-7; ⊙9am-7pm Mon-Sat; ⧫Sant'Angelo)

Cavatappi

OSTERIA, CICHETI BAR €€

15 Map p34, G2

A casual charmer offering *cicheti* and artisanal cheeses, DOC bubbly by the glass, and that rarest of San Marco finds: a tasty sit-down meal under €20. Get the risotto of the day and an ultrafresh salad with toasted hazlenuts – and if your dinner date is exceptionally worthy, share the warm sheep's cheese drizzled with Dolomite wildflower honey. (☑041 296 02 52; Campo della Guerra 525/526; cicheti €2-4, meals €25-40; ⊙10am-9pm Tue-Thu & Sun, to 11pm Fri & Sat; ⧨; ⧫San Marco)

Osteria da Carla

OSTERIA, CICHETI BAR €

16 Map p34, F4

For the price of hot chocolate in Piazza San Marco, diners in the know duck into this hidden courtyard to feast on handmade ravioli with poppyseed, pear and sheep's cheese. Expect a wait at lunch and happy hour, when *gondolieri* abandon ship for DOC soave and *sopressa crostini* (soft salami on toast). (☑ 041 523 78 55; Frezzaria 1535; meals €20-25; ☺10am-9pm Mon-Sat; ☺Vallaresso)

Rosa Salva

BAKERY €

17 Map p34, F2

With just-baked strudel and reliably frothy cappuccino, Rosa Salva has provided Venetians with fresh reasons to roll out of bed for over a century. Cheerfully efficient staff working the spotless granite counter ensure that no *curasan* (croissant) order waits for more than a minute, and supply

---

✅ Top Tip

Coffee or Rent?

In San Marco the price of a sit-down coffee seems more like rent. Take your coffee standing at a bar for €1 to €2.50, spend a couple more euros for an outside table, or luxuriate inside baroque cafes in Piazza San Marco. There's usually a €6 music surcharge for outdoor seats in Piazza San Marco.

---

gale-force espresso and turbo-loaded chocolate profiteroles to power you across 30 more bridges. (☑ 041 522 79 34; www.rosasalva.it; Mercerie 5020; pastries €1.10-2.80; ☺7.30am-8pm Thu-Tue; ☑ ☺; ☺Rialto)

Drinking

I Rusteghi

WINE BAR

18 Map p34, F1

Honouring centuries of Venetian *enoteca* tradition, fourth-generation sommelier Giovanni d'Este will open any bottle on his shelves to pour you an *ombra* (half-glass of wine) – including collector's wines like Cannubi Barolo. Request *'qualcosa di particolare'* (something exceptional) and Giovanni will reward you with a sensual Ribolla Gialla to pair with truffle-cheese mini-*panini* and platters of Spanish and Veneto ham. (☑ 041 523 22 05; www.osteriairusteghi.com; Corte del Tentor 5513; mini-panini €2-5; ☺10.30am-3pm & 6-11.30pm Mon-Sat; ☺Rialto)

Harry's Bar

BAR

19 Map p34, F5

Aspiring auteurs hold court at bistro tables well scuffed by Ernest Hemingway, Charlie Chaplin, Truman Capote and Orson Welles, enjoying the signature €16.50 bellini (Giuseppe Cipriani's original 1948 recipe: white-peach juice and *prosecco*) with a side of reflected glory. Upstairs is one of Italy's most unaccountably expensive restaurants – stick to the bar to save financing for your breakthrough film. (☎041 528 57 77; Calle Vallaresso 1323; cocktails €12-22; ☺10.30am-11pm; 🚊San Marco)

Teamo

CAFE, BAR

20 Map p34, D3

Sunny tearoom by day, sleek backlit alabaster bar by night (and fabulous full time). Arrive by 6.30pm for first choice of fresh *cicheti* at the bar and lookers in the leather banquettes –

☑ Top Tip

Backstreet Routes

On average, Venetians get asked once daily for directions to tourist destinations like Piazza San Marco, Rialto, Accademia and Ferrovia (the train station) – and if you stay awhile and walk confidently, you'll be asked too. Dodge the day-tripper crowds by taking alternative routes to your destination along minor *calli* (backstreets) that wiggle through quieter Venetian neighbourhoods, often in approximate parallel with major thoroughfares like Strada Nuova (Rialto–Ferrovia), Marzaria (San Marco–Rialto) and Calle Larga XXII Marzo (San Marco–Accademia). Favourite local bypass routes are **Calle dei Fabbri** (San Marco–Rialto, behind Caffè Quadri) and **Piscina Frezzeria** (San Marco–Accademia, near La Fenice).

this bar swings both ways, so there's something for everyone. (☎347 549 90 82; Rio Terà della Mandola 3795; ☺8am-10pm; 🚊Sant'Angelo)

Torino@Notte

BAR

21 Map p34, E2

Freeform, eclectic and loud, by day Torino is a cafe, but after 7pm locals roll in for €2 to €5 drinks and marathon DJ sessions of vintage reggae and soul on vinyl. Stop by Friday and Saturday after 9pm for a late bite or nightcap with live jazz, blues or rock. (☎041 522 39 14; Campo San Luca 4592; ☺7pm-1am Tue-Sat; 🚊Rialto)

Caffè Quadri

CAFE, BAR

22 Map p34, G3

Powdered wigs seem appropriate in this baroque cafe, serving royal happy hours since 1638. The upstairs restaurant charges a king's ransom for finicky fare upstaged by Piazza San Marco views, but the gilded downstairs cafe serves a princely €12 hot chocolate with *panna* (whipped cream). Reserve ahead during Carnevale, when costumed Quadri revellers party like it's 1699. (☎041 522 21 05; www.alajmo.it; Piazza San Marco 120; drinks €6-25; ☺9am-11.30pm; 🚊San Marco)

Osteria All'Alba

WINE BAR

23 Map p34, F1

That roar behind the Rialto means the DJ's funk set is kicking in at

All'Alba. Squeeze inside to order salami sandwiches (€1 to €2.50) and DOC Veneto wines (€5 to €6), and check out walls festooned with vintage LPs and effusive thanks scrawled in 12 languages. (📞340 124 56 34; Ramo del Fontego dei Tedeschi 5370; ⏰10am-1am; 🚤Rialto)

Caffè Centrale
LOUNGE

24 🍸 Map p34, E4

Under moody Murano-chandelier lighting, you might spot Salma Hayek, Spike Lee and sundry America's Cup sailors within these exposed-brick walls. Meals are pricey and canalside VIP tables chilly, but Centrale draws La Fenice post-opera crowds with signature foamy *spritz* (*prosecco* and bitters cocktails), midnight snacks, chill-out DJ sets and occasional live jazz. (📞041 296 06 64; www.caffecentrale venezia.com; Piscina Frezzaria 1659b; drinks €3.50-15; ⏰7pm-2am Wed-Mon; 🚤San Marco)

Entertainment

Teatro La Fenice
OPERA

25 ⭐ Map p34, D4

A €90 million replica of the 19th-century opera house reopened in 2003, after it burned down in 1996. Tours are possible with advance booking (📞041 24 24), but the best way to see La Fenice is with the *loggione* – opera buffs who pass judgment from the top-tier cheap seats. When the opera is in recess, look for symphonies and chamber-music concerts. (📞041 78 65 11; www.teatrolafenice.it; Campo San Fantin 1965; theatre visits adult/reduced €8.50/6, opera tickets from €40; ⏰tours 9.30am-6pm; 🚤Santa Maria del Giglio)

Teatro Goldoni
THEATRE

26 ⭐ Map p34, E2

Named after the city's great playwright, Venice's main theatre has an impressive dramatic range that runs from Goldoni's comedy to Shakespearean tragedy (mostly in Italian), plus ballets and concerts. Don't be fooled by the huge modern Brutalist bronze doors: this venerable theatre dates from 1622, and the jewel-box interior seats just 800. (📞041 240 20 14; www.teatrostabileveneto.it; Calle Teatro Goldoni 4650b; tickets €8-29; ⏰box office 10am-1pm & 3-7.30pm Mon-Fri; 🚤Rialto)

Multisala Rossini
CINEMA

27 ⭐ Map p34, D3

Film buffs who miss the proverbial boat to the annual Venice Film Festival on the Lido, rejoice: award-winning films and blockbusters screen year-round at the city's newest and largest cinema. Sala 1 is the largest of three screening rooms, with seating for 300 and excellent sound. Some films are screened in the original language, but most are dubbed in Italian. (📞041 241 72 74; Calle San Benedetto 3997a; adult/reduced €7.50/6, 3D films €10/9; ⏰shows Tue-Sun; ♿; 🚤Rialto)

Understand

Keeping Venice Afloat

Impossible though it seems, Venetians built their home on 117 small islands connected by some 400 bridges over 150 canals. But if floating marble palaces boggle the mind, consider what's underneath them: an entire forest's worth of petrified wood pylons, rammed through silty *barene* (shoals) into the clay lagoon floor.

Venice is ingeniously constructed to contend with lagoon tides, so even a four-alarm *acqua alta* (exceptionally high tide) is rarely cause for panic. But on 4 November 1966, record floods poured into 16,000 Venetian homes in terrifying waves, and residents were stranded in the wreckage of 1400 years of civilisation. Thanks to Venice's international appeal, assistance poured in and Unesco coordinated 50 private organisations to redress the ravages of the flood.

Cleaning up after *acqua alta* is a tedious job for Venetians: pumping water out of flooded ground floors and preventing corrosion by scrubbing salt residue off surfaces. Venice's canals must also be regularly dredged, which involves pumping water out, removing pungent sludge, then patching brickwork by hand with a ticklish technique Venetians call *scuci-cuci*.

Deep channels dug to accommodate tankers and cruise ships allow more seawater into the lagoon, changing aquaculture and elevating high tides. The multi-billion-euro mobile flood barrier known as Mose is intended to limit *acqua alta*, but critics question its effectiveness, environmental impact and diversion of funds critical for Venice's upkeep.

Venice and its lagoon are a Unesco World Heritage site – but in the wake of Tuscany's 2012 *Costa Concordia* shipwreck, Unesco expressed concern about the impact of cruise ships. Italy's Port Authority has proposed rerouting cruise ships to Venice via inland Porta Marghera, bypassing Giudecca Canal. But critics like Venice's No Grandi Navi (No Big Ships) committee oppose cruise-ship entry into the lagoon due to pollution, including canalbank-corroding sulphur waste. Alternative seaward ports have been proposed at Malamocco.

Meanwhile, responsible travelers are taking action – eating sustainably sourced, local food; conserving water; using products free of industrial chemicals; and above all, supporting local businesses – which help to offset tourism impact, and keep Venice afloat.

Shopping

Chiarastella Cattana
ARTISANAL, HOMEWARES

28 🔒 Map p34, B3

Transform any home into a thoroughly modern *palazzo* with these locally woven, strikingly original Venetian linens. Whimsical cushions feature a chubby purple rhinoceros and grumpy scarlet elephants straight out of Pietro Longhi paintings, and hand-tasseled Venetian jacquard hand towels will dry your royal guests in style. Decorators and design aficionados, save an afternoon to consider dizzying woven-to-order napkin and curtain options here. (☎041 522 43 69; www.chiarastellacattana.it; Salizada San Samuele 3357; ⏱10am-1pm & 3-7pm Mon-Sat; ⛴San Samuele)

Malefatte
ARTISANAL, ACCESSORIES

29 🔒 Map p34, C4

'Misdeeds' is the name of this non-profit initiative by and for incarcerated workers, but its pop-art man-bags made from recycled-vinyl museum banners are clever indeed. T-shirts showing *acqua alta* measurements and aprons silk screened with the *spritz* recipe are souvenirs with a difference: all proceeds support training and transitions from jail on Giudecca to new lives and productive careers in Venice. (www.rioteradeipensieri.org; Campo Santo Stefano kiosk; ⏱10.30am-5.30pm Tue-Sat; ⛴Accademia)

Fiorella Gallery
FASHION

30 🔒 Map p34, C4

Groupies are the only accessory needed to go with Fiorella's silk-velvet smoking jackets in louche lavender and oxblood, printed by hand with skulls, peacocks or a Fiorella signature: wide-eyed rats. Shock-frock coats starting in the mid-three figures make Alexander McQueen seem retro – Fiorella's been pioneering rebel couture since 1968. Hours are approximate; as the sign says: 'We open sometime'. (☎041 520 92 28; www.fiorellagallery.com; Campo Santo Stefano 2806; ⏱9.30am-1.30pm & 3.30-7pm Tue-Sat, 3-7pm Mon; ⛴Accademia)

Ottica Carraro
EYEWEAR

31 🔒 Map p34, D3

Lost your sunglasses on the Lido? Never fear: Ottica Carraro can make you a custom pair within 24 hours, including the eye exam. The store has its own limited-edition 'Venice' line, ranging from cat-eye shades perfect for facing paparazzi to chunky wood-grain frames that could get you mistaken for an art critic at the Biennale. (☎041 520 42 58; www.otticacarraro.it; Calle della Mandola 3706; ⏱9am-1pm & 3-7.30pm Mon-Sat; ⛴Sant'Angelo)

Godi Fiorenza
ARTISANAL, FASHION

32 🔒 Map p34, E3

Impeccably tailored, midnight-blue silk-satin dresses with exuberant woolly shoulders showcase the Saville

RICHARD I'ANSON / GETTY IMAGES ©

Venetian glass

Row skills of sisters Patrizia and Samanta Fiorenza, but also their vivid imaginations – their latest collection was inspired by men's tuxedos and deconstructed teddy bears. They specialise in couture at off-the-rack prices: for under €100, hand-beaded antique-lace collars add turn-of-the-century elegance to modern minimalism. (☏041 241 08 66; Rio Tera San Paternian 4261; ☉9.30am-6.30pm Mon-Sat; 🚤Rialto)

Arnoldo & Battois
FASHION, ACCESSORIES

33 🔒 Map p34, E3

Handbags become heirlooms in the hands of Venetian designers Massimiliano Battois and Silvano Arnoldo, whose handcrafted clutches come in bold, buttery turquoise and magenta leather with baroque closures in laser-cut wood. Artfully draped emerald and graphite silk dresses complete the look for Biennale openings. (☏041 528 59 44; www.arnoldoebattois.com; Calle dei Fuseri 4271; ☉10am-1pm & 3.30-7pm Mon-Thu & Sat; 🚤Rialto)

Caigo da Mar
HOME & GARDEN

34 🔒 Map p34, B4

Venetian pirates once headed to Constantinople for all their interior-decoration needs, but today they'd need look no further than this tiny treasure trove. It brims with dramatic black Murano glass candleabras and a designer booty of Fornasetti cushions, plus enough octopus-shaped lamps and nautilus-shell dishes to make any living room look like the lost city of Atlantis. (☎041 243 32 38; www .caigodamar.com; Calle delle Botteghe 3131; ◷11am-1pm & 4-7pm Mon-Fri, 11am-7pm Sat; ☕Accademia)

Pagine e Cuoio　ARTISANAL, LEATHER

35 🔒　Map p34, E4

The lion of San Marco looks fashionably fierce embossed upon a turquoise billfold by leather artisan Davide Desanzuane. Unexpected colours update Venetian heraldry for the 21st century on Desanzuane's tablet cases, smartphone carriers and business-card holders – and since they're all one of a kind, they make singular fashion statements. (☎041 528 65 55; Calle del Fruttariol 1845; ◷9.30am-7pm Mon-Sat; ☕Santa Maria del Giglio)

Le Botteghe della Solidarietà　GIFTS, HOMEWARES

36 🔒　Map p34, F1

Italian design sensibilities meet Venetian trading smarts at this fair-trade boutique on the steps of the Rialto. Gondola rides call for straw hats woven by a Bangladeshi collective and refreshing Libera Terra wine from vineyards reclaimed from the mafia, while kids are placated by organic chocolate and recycled cans fashioned into toy Vespas. (☎041 522 75 45; www .coopfilo.it; Salizada Pio X 5164; ◷10am-7pm Mon-Sat; ☕Rialto)

Esperienze　GLASS, JEWELLERY

37 🔒　Map p34, G2

When an Italian minimalist falls in love with a Murano glassblower, the result is spare, spirited glass jewellery. Esperienze is a collaborative effort for husband-wife team Graziano and Sara: he breathes life into her designs, including matte-glass teardrop pendants and cracked-ice earrings. Their mutual admiration for Guggenheim Collection modernists shows in colourful necklaces that resemble Calder mobiles and Kandinsky paintings. (☎041 521 29 45; www.esperienzevenezia .com; Calle degli Specchieri 473b; ◷10am-noon & 3-7pm; ☕San Marco)

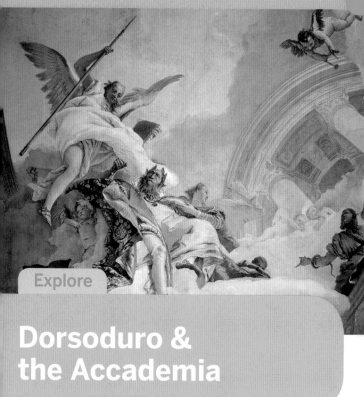

Explore

Dorsoduro & the Accademia

Dorsoduro covers prime Grand Canal waterfront with Gallerie dell'Accademia's Renaissance beauty, Ca' Rezzonico's gilded splendour, Peggy Guggenheim Collection's modernism and Punta della Dogana's contemporary installation art. Locals sunbathe and stroll along the Zattere waterfront on sunny days, and convene nightly in Campo Santa Margherita for cocktails and conversation.

The Sights in a Day

☼ Brace yourself with cappuccino at **Il Caffè Rosso** (p55) for an epic journey through eight centuries of Venetian masterpieces at **Gallerie dell'Accademia** (p50). Afterwards, recover your senses over canalside *panini* (sandwiches) at **Cantinone Già Schiavi** (p63).

☀ See Pollock spatter-paintings and Calder mobiles make a splash along the Grand Canal at the Peggy Guggenheim Collection, then argue the merits of Jeff Koons and other controversial installation art at **Punta della Dogana** (p58). Let the mysterious powers of **Basilica di Santa Maria della Salute** (p58) restore your peace of mind, before it's boggled by Vedova's robotic art displays at **Magazzini del Sale** (p60) and Veronese's floor-to-ceiling masterpieces at **Chiesa di San Sebastian** (p58).

☾ Enjoy dinner at **Ristorante La Bitta** (p60) before or after your hot concert date – whether that's a baroque concerto in frescoed **Ca' Rezzonico** (p58), opera at Tiepolo-ceilinged **Scuola Grande dei Carmini** (p59) or swing at **Venice Jazz Club** (p64).

For a local's day in Dorsoduro, see p54.

Top Sights

Gallerie dell'Accademia (p50)

Peggy Guggenheim Collection (p52)

◯ Local Life

Happy Hour in Campo Santa Margherita (p54)

♥ Best of Venice

Museums

Gallerie dell'Accademia (p50)

Peggy Guggenheim Collection (p52)

Ca' Rezzonico (p58)

Punta della Dogana (p58)

Magazzini del Sale (p60)

Drinking

Il Caffè Rosso (p55)

Cantina di Millevini (p55)

Getting There

🚤 **Vaporetto** Grand Canal 1, 2 and N lines stop at Accademia; line 1 also calls at Ca' Rezzonico and Salute. Lines 51, 52, 61, 62 and the N night *vaporetto* (passenger ferry) call at the Zattere and/or San Basilio. Airport lines also head to the Zattere stop.

Top Sights
Gallerie dell'Accademia

Hardly academic, these galleries contain more murderous intrigue, forbidden romance and shameless politicking than the most outrageous Venetian parties. The former Santa Maria della Carità convent complex maintained its serene composure for centuries, but ever since Napoleon installed his haul of Venetian art trophies in 1807, there's been nonstop visual drama inside these walls. Note that last admission is 45 minutes before closing.

◉ Map p56, E4

gallerieaccademia.org

Campo della Carità 1050

adult/reduced/EU child & senior €14/11/free

🕘8.15am-2pm Mon, to 7.15pm Tue-Sun

🚤Accademia

Interior, Gallerie dell'Accademia

Don't Miss

Carpaccio
UFO arrivals seem imminent in the glowing skies of Carpaccio's gruesome *Crucifixion* and *Glorification of the Ten Thousand Martyrs of Mount Ararat* (Room 2).

Tintoretto
The Venetian Renaissance master's *Creation of the Animals* (Room 6) is a fantastical bestiary suggesting God put forth his best efforts inventing Venetian seafood (no argument here).

Titian
His 1576 *Pietà* (Room 6) was possibly finished posthumously by Palma il Giovane, but notice the smears of paint Titian applied with his bare hands and the column-base self-portrait.

Veronese
Paolo Veronese's freshly restored *Feast in the House of Levi* (Room 10) was originally called Last Supper, until Inquisition leaders condemned it for showing dogs and drunkards, among others, cavorting with Apostles. Veronese refused to change a thing besides the title.

Portrait Galleries
Lock eyes with Lorenzo Lotto's soul-searching *Portrait of a Young Scholar,* Rosalba Carriera's brutally honest self-portrait and Pietro Longhi's lovestruck violinist in *The Dance Lesson.*

Sala dell'Albergo
The Accademia's grand finale is the newly restored Sala dell'Albergo, with a lavishly carved ceiling, Antonio Vivarini's wrap-around 1441–50 masterpiece of fluffy-bearded saints, and Titian's 1534–39 *Presentation of the Virgin.*

☑ Top Tips

▸ To skip ahead of the queues in high season, book tickets online (booking fee €1.50).

▸ Queues are shorter in the afternoon; last entry is 45 minutes before closing, but proper visits take at least 90 minutes.

▸ Leave large items behind or you'll have to drop them off at the baggage depot (€0.50 per piece).

▸ An audio guide (€5) is available but is mostly descriptive and largely unnecessary – avoid the wait and follow your bliss and explanatory wall tags.

▸ Bathrooms are elegantly restored in spotless marble, so there's no need to pay €1 for iffy public restrooms outside.

✖ Take a Break

Gourmets and starving artists converge on Bar alla Toletta (p62) for grilled-to-order *panini,* generously packed with specialty cheeses and cured meats.

Top Sights
Peggy Guggenheim Collection

After tragically losing her father on the *Titanic*, heiress Peggy Guggenheim befriended Dadaists, dodged Nazis and changed art history at her palatial home on the Grand Canal. Peggy's Palazzo Venier dei Leoni is a showcase for surrealism, futurism and abstract expressionism by some 200 breakthrough modern artists, including Peggy's ex-husband Max Ernst and Jackson Pollock (among her many rumoured lovers).

👁 Map p56, F4

guggenheim-venice.it

Palazzo Venier dei Leoni 704

adult/senior/reduced €14/11/8

🕙10am-6pm Wed-Mon

🚤Accademia

Peggy Guggenheim Collection building, Grand Canal

Don't Miss

Modernist Collection

Peggy Guggenheim escaped Paris two days before the Nazi invasion, and boldly defied established social and artistic dictates. She collected according to her own convictions, featuring folk art and lesser-known artists alongside such radical early modernists as Kandinsky, Picasso, Man Ray, Rothko, Mondrian, Joseph Cornell and Dalí.

Italian Avant-Garde

Upon her 1948 arrival in Venice, Peggy became a spirited advocate for contemporary Italian art, which had largely gone out of favour with the rise of Mussolini and the partisan politics of WWII. Her support led to reappraisals of Umberto Boccioni, Giorgio Morandi, Giacomo Balla, Giuseppe Capogrossi and Giorgio de Chirico, and aided Venice's own Emilio Vedova and Giuseppe Santomaso. Never afraid to make a splash, Peggy gave passing gondoliers an eyeful on her Grand Canal quay: Marino Marini's 1948 *Angel of the City*, a bronze male nude on horseback visibly excited by the possibilities on the horizon.

Sculpture Garden

Peggy's palace was never finished, but that didn't stop her from filling every space indoors and out with art. In the sculpture garden, wander past bronzes by Henry Moore, Alberto Giacometti and Constantin Brancusci; Yoko Ono's *Wish Tree* and a shiny black-granite lump by Anish Kapoor. The city of Venice granted an honorary dispensation for Peggy Guggenheim to be buried beneath the Giacometti sculptures, alongside her dearly departed lapdogs.

☑ **Top Tips**

▶ Save a few euro on admission to the Peggy Guggenheim Collection by bringing your Trenitalia or Alitalia ticket to the museum. The offer is good for new arrivals with train tickets no more than three days old, and Alitalia airline passengers with tickets up to seven days old.

▶ The garden pavilion houses a bookshop, cafe, bathrooms and temporary exhibits highlighting underappreciated modernist rebels.

▶ Around the corner from the museum on Fondamenta Venier dei Leoni, a larger museum shop sells art books in several languages and replicas of Peggy's signature glasses – winged, like the lion of San Marco.

✘ **Take a Break**

The garden pavilion's veranda cafe offers respectable espresso and views over the sculpture gardens.

Local Life
Happy Hour in Campo Santa Margherita

By day Campo Santa Margherita hosts a weekday fish market, the odd flea market and periodic political protests, but by six o'clock this unruly square becomes Venice's nightlife hub. Just don't try to pack it all into one happy hour. Pace yourself on your *giro d'ombra* (pub crawl), lest you end up in the drink of a nearby canal.

❶ Snacks at Ai Do Draghi

'Permesso!' (Pardon!) is the chorus inside this historic **bar** (☎041 528 97 31; Calle della Chiesa 3665; ⏱7.30am-10pm Fri-Wed; 🚤Ca' Rezzonico), where the crowd spills onto the sidewalk and tries not to spill drinks in the process. Arrive at the tiny wooden bar early for the best choice of 45-plus wines by the glass and respectable *tramezzini* (sandwiches).

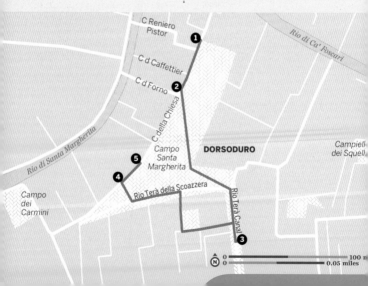

❷ Spritz at Il Caffè Rosso

Locals affectionately call this red **storefront** (☎041 528 79 98; Campo Santa Margherita 2963; ⏰7am-1am Mon-Sat; 🚤Ca' Rezzonico) *'al rosso'* (the red), and its inexpensive *spritz* (*prosecco* and bitters cocktail) generously splashed with Aperol gives visitors and locals alike an instant flush of Venetian colour. Plan to arrive when the clock strikes '*spritz* o'clock' at 6pm sharp, and mingle with standing-room-only crowds.

❸ Cocktails at Imagina Café

For your next stop, branch out to top-shelf cocktails served at this sleek, backlit **bar** (☎041 241 06 25; www.imaginacafe.it; Rio Terà Canal 3126; ⏰8am-2am Mon-Sat; ♿; 🚤Ca' Rezzonico) surrounded by local art. The creative, chatty and gay-friendly crowd here should probably start paying rent at outdoor tables, while their sweater-clad dogs bask in the admiration of passers-by.

❹ Wining & Dining at Cantina di Millevini

Before the next round of drinks, grab a table indoors on the piazza for soothing soups, salads and fish carpaccio of the day (€6.50 to €10). This respected Venetian **wine merchant** (Millevini in Campo; ☎041 522 34 36; www .millevini.it; Campo Santa Margherita 3026; ⏰3pm-midnight Mon-Sat; 🚤Ca' Rezzonico) offers inspired pairings from bottle-lined brick walls and a select menu of DOC, biodynamic and organic Veneto vintages by the glass.

❺ Midnight Merlot at Osteria alla Bifora

While *spritz*-pounding students carouse outside in the *campo*, gentle flirting ensues in this chandelier-lit medieval **wine cave** (☎041 523 61 19; Campo Santa Margherita 2930; ⏰noon-3pm & 6pm-1am Wed-Mon; 🚤Ca' Rezzonico) over big-hearted Veneto merlot. While you wait for a midnight-snack platter of cheese and carved-to-order cured meats to arrive, you'll make new friends at communal tables.

0   200 m
0.1 miles

Sant' Angelo

San Tomà

C degli Avvocati

C Pesaro

Corte dell'Alberto

Rio di Sant'Angelo

Rio de Ca'Garzoni

C d'Caffettier

C dei Assassini

Rio della Verona

C d Barcaroli

Rio di Ca' Bernardo

amo Lezze

Saliz S Samuele

delle Carrozze

Saliz Malipiero

C dei Orbi

C d Muneghe

C de Pestrin

Campo S Angelo

C Caotorta

C della Fenice

Piscina Frezzaria

C del Carro

C dei Frati

SAN MARCO

Rio Malatin

Rio della Veste

Campo Santo Stefano

Campo S Maurizio

Fond Corner Zaguri

Rio di San Maurizio

C delle Ostreghe

Campo Traghetto

C Larga

C del Squero

C del Pestrin

C del Traghetto

Campo di San Moisè

Corte Barozzi

Rio del Duca

C Vitturi

C Giustinian

Campo di S Vidal

C delle Dose

C Gritti

Rio dell'Orso

Accademia

Campo della Carità

Gallerie dell'Accademia

Santa Maria del Giglio

Fond Dogana alla Salute

Salute

Punta della Dogana

4

Campo della Salute

Piscina Forner

Campo San Vio

C S Cristoforo

C d Chiesa

21

Fond Ospedaletto

28

C d Bastion

Peggy Guggenheim Collection

Fond della Salute

Rio della Salute

C del Squero

Basilica di Santa Maria della Salute

2

C Pompea

C Franchi

Corte Nova

C Molin

Ruo Terra del Spezier

C da

Fond Venier

C C Capuzzi

Fond Soranzo della Fornace

Piscina Venier

C C Bragadin

Rio Terà di San Vio

C degli Incurabili

C delle Turette

Rio della Fornace

Rio di San Vio

C d Squero

Magazzini del Sale

Bala

7

Fond Zattere Santo Spirito

5

Sights

Ca' Rezzonico
MUSEUM

 Map p56, D2

Baroque dreams come true at Baldassare Longhena's palace, where a marble staircase leads to gilded ballrooms, frescoed salons and sumptuous boudoirs. Giambattista Tiepolo's Throne Room ceiling is a masterpiece of elegant social climbing: Merit ascends to the Temple of Glory with the Golden Book of Venetian nobles' names – including Tiepolo's patrons, the Rezzonico family. (Museum of the 18th Century; ☎041 241 01 00; www.visitmuve.it; Fondamenta Rezzonico 3136; adult/reduced €8/5.50, or Museum Pass; ⏱10am-6pm Wed-Mon Apr-Oct, to 5pm Nov-Mar; 🚤Ca' Rezzonico)

Basilica di Santa Maria della Salute
CHURCH

 Map p56, H4

Commissioned by Venice's plague survivors as thanks for salvation,

---

Top Tip

Salute Vespers

If you think Longhena's dome looks magnificent, wait until you hear how it sounds. Weekdays at 3.30pm, vespers are played on Basilica di Santa Maria della Salute's original 1782–83 organ. These musical interludes are free, and the acoustics are suitably heavenly.

Baldassare Longhena's uplifting design is an engineering feat that defies simple logic; in fact, the church is said to have mystical curative properties. Titian eluded the plague until age 90, leaving a legacy of masterpieces now in Salute's sacristy. (La Salute; ☎041 241 10 18; www.seminariovenezia.it; Campo della Salute 1b; admission free, sacristy adult/reduced €3/1.50; ⏱9am-noon & 3-5.30pm; 🚤Salute)

Chiesa di San Sebastian
CHURCH

 Map p56, A3

A hidden treasure of Venetian art, this otherwise humble church was embellished with floor-to-ceiling masterpieces by Paolo Veronese over three decades. Antonio Scarpignano's relatively austere 1508–48 facade creates a sense of false modesty from the outside, because inside the restored interior decor goes wild. (www.chorusvenezia.org; Campo San Sebastiano 1687; admission €3, or with Chorus Pass; ⏱10am-5pm Mon-Sat; 🚤San Basilio)

Punta della Dogana
ART GALLERY

4 Map p56, H4

Fortuna, the weathervane atop Punta della Dogana, swung Venice's way in 2005, when billionaire art collector François Pinault decided to showcase his artworks in abandoned warehouses at Punta della Dogana. Massive installations address deeply personal fixations, including Chen Zhen's pure crystal versions of his diseased internal organs and Abdel Abdessemed's drawings of Molotov-cocktail throwers

Punta della Dogana

propped on concert stands to create orchestrated violence. (☎041 271 90 39; www.palazzograssi.it; adult/reduced/child €15/10/free, incl Palazzo Grassi €20/15/free; ⏱10am-7pm Wed-Mon; ⛴Salute)

Scuola Grande dei Carmini
HISTORICAL BUILDING

5 ◉ Map p56, B2

Eighteenth-century backpackers must have thought they'd died and gone to heaven at Scuola Grande dei Carmini, with its lavish interiors by Giambattista Tiepolo and Baldassare Longhena. Longhena designed the gold-leafed stucco stairway to heaven, glimpsed upstairs in Tiepolo's nine-panel ceiling *Virgin in Glory*. The adjoining hostel room is bedecked in *boiserie* (wood carving). (☎041 528 94 20; www.scuola grandecarmini.it; Campo Santa Margherita 2617; adult/reduced €5/4; ⏱11am-4pm; ⛴Ca' Rezzonico)

Chiesa dei Gesuati
CHURCH

6 ◉ Map p56, D5

There's year-round sunshine inside Giorgio Massari's baroque church. Luminous skies surrounding St Dominic in Tiepolo's 1737–39 ceiling frescoes are so convincing, you'll wonder whether you're wearing enough sunscreen. Tintoretto's sombre 1565 *Crucifixion* shows Mary fainting with grief – but Sebastiano Ricci's cherubs perform comical tumbling routines in 1730–33 *Saints Peter and Thomas with Pope Pius V*. (Church of Santa Maria del

Rosario; www.chorusvenezia.org; Fondamenta delle Zattere 918; admission €3, or Chorus Pass; ⏰10am-5pm Mon-Sat; ⛴Zattere)

Magazzini del Sale ART GALLERY

7 Map p56, G5

A recent retrofit designed by Pritzker Prize–winning architect Renzo Piano transformed Venice's historical salt warehouses into Fondazione Vedova art galleries, commemorating pioneering Venetian abstract painter Emilio Vedova. Fondazione Vedova shows are often literally moving and rotating: powered by renewable energy sources, 10 robotic arms designed by Vedova and Piano move major modern artworks in and out of storage slots. (☎041 522 66 26; www.fondazionevedova.org; Zattere 266; donation suggested during shows; ⏰during shows 10.30am-6pm Wed-Mon; ⛴Zattere)

Local Life
Squero San Trovaso

The **wood cabin** (Map p56, C4; Campo San Trovaso 1097) along Rio di San Trovaso may look like a stray ski chalet, but it's one of Venice's three working *squeri* (shipyards), with refinished gondolas drying in the yard. When the door's open, you can peek inside in exchange for a donation left in the can by the door. To avoid startling gondola-builders working with sharp tools, no flash photography is allowed.

Eating

Ristorante La Bitta RISTORANTE €€

8 Map p56, C3

The daily menu arrives on an artist's easel, and the hearty rustic fare looks like a still life and tastes like a carnivore's dream: steak comes snugly wrapped in bacon, and roast rabbit tops marinated rocket. This bistro focuses on local meats – *'bitta'* means 'mooring post' – and seats only 35. Reservations essential; cash only. (☎041 523 05 31; Calle Lunga San Barnaba 2753a; meals €30-40; ⏰dinner Mon-Sat; ⛴Ca' Rezzonico)

Enoteca Ai Artisti RISTORANTE €€€

9 Map p56, C3

Indulgent cheeses, exceptional *nero di seppia* (cuttlefish ink) pasta, and tender *tagliata* (sliced steak) drizzled with aged balsamic vinegar atop arugula are paired with exceptional wines by the glass by your oenophile hosts. Pavement tables for two make great people-watching, but book ahead for indoor tables for groups as space is limited. (☎041 523 89 44; www.enotecaartisti.com; Fondamenta della Toletta 1169a; meals €40-50; ⏰noon-4pm & 6.30-10pm Mon-Sat; ⛴Ca' Rezzonico)

Grom GELATERIA €

10 Map p56, C3

Lick the landscape at Grom, featuring Slow Food ingredients from across Italy: lemon from the Amalfi Coast, pistachio from Sicily, hazelnuts from Piedmont. Fair-trade chocolate and coffee-sourcing helped win the Turin-based Grom chain a 'Master of Slow Food' designation, but with seasonal flavours ranging from chestnut cream to apricot sorbet, you might award it another honorary title: lunch. (☑041 099 17 51; www.grom.it; Campo San Barnaba 2461; gelati €2.50-4; ⏰11am-midnight Sun-Thu, to 1am Fri & Sat; 👶; 🚤Ca' Rezzonico)

Antica Trattoria La Furatola
VENETIAN, SEAFOOD €€€

11 🍴 Map p56, B3

Before becoming museum central, Dorsoduro was a fishermen's neighbourhood where the *furatola* (provisioner) offered simple, honest fare. La Furatola has gone upmarket but still dishes seafood to Venetian fishermen's standards, fresh from the Pescaria. Seafood appetisers are main events with *canoce* (mantis prawn), followed by handmade pastas – go Sunday for ravioli *alla busara* (with prawn sauce). Cash only. (☑041 520 85 94; Calle Lunga San Barnaba 2870a; meals €40-60; ⏰12.30-2.30pm & 7.30-10.30pm Tue-Wed & Fri-Sun, 7.30-10.30pm Thu; 🚤Ca' Rezzonico)

Pasticceria Tonolo
PASTRIES, CAKES €

12 🍴 Map p56, C1

Dire B&B breakfasts with packaged croissants are corrected at Tonolo, which serves flaky *apfelstrudel* (apple pastry), velvety *bignè al zabaione* (marsala cream pastry) and oozing *pain au chocolat* (choco-

Enoteca Ai Artisti

late croissants). Chocolate-topped beignets are filled with hazelnut mousse as rich as a Venetian doge at tax time. (☑041 532 72 09; Calle dei Preti 3764; pastries €1-3; ⏰7.45am-8pm Tue-Sat, 8am-1pm Sun; 🚤San Tomá)

Impronta Café
ITALIAN €

13 🍴 Map p56, C1

Join Venice's value-minded jet set for *prosecco* (Venetian sparkling wine) and bargain polenta-salami combos, surrounded by witty architectural diagrams of cooking pots. When other restaurants close, Impronta accommodates late lunches, teatime with a wide tea selection, and midnight

PIERE BONBON / ALAMY ©

Ristorante La Bitta (p60)

snacks of club sandwiches – yet somehow, the staff remains chipper and the bathroom spotless. (☎041 275 03 86; Calle Crosera 3815; meals €8-15; ☺7am-2am Mon-Sat; 🚻; 🚤San Tomà)

Pane Vino e San Daniele

ITALIAN €€

14 🍴 Map p56, B3

Artists can't claim they're starving any more after a meal in this wood-beamed trattoria, a favourite of art students and professors alike. Settle in to generous plates of gnocchi laced with truffle cheese, Veneto game such as roast rabbit and duck, lavish appetisers featuring the namesake San Daniele cured ham, and Friulian house wines made by the Fantinel

family owners. (☎041 243 98 65; www .panevinovenice.com; Calle Lunga San Barnaba 2861; meals €15-30; ☺10am-2pm Tue-Sun; 🚤Ca' Rezzonico)

Bar alla Toletta

SANDWICHES €

15 🍴 Map p56, C3

Midway through museum crawls from Accademia to Ca' Rezzonico, Bar Toletta satisfies starving customers with creative, grilled-to-order *panini,* including ham with fresh porcini and daily vegetarian options. *Tramezzini* (triangular, stacked sandwiches made with squishy white bread) are tasty, too – Bar Toletta goes easy on mayonnaise in favour of more flavourful toppings like olive tapenade. Have a seat for €0.50 extra per sandwich, or get yours to go. (☏041 520 01 96; Calle la Toletta 1192; sandwiches €1.50-6; ☺8am-8pm Mon-Sat; 🖉🚻; 🚤Ca' Rezzonico)

Drinking

Cantinone Già Schiavi BAR

16 Map p56, D4

Chaos cheerfully prevails at this legendary canalside spot, where Accademia art historians rub shoulders with San Trovaso gondola builders with not a drop spilled. Don't miss out on tuna-leek *cicheti* (Venetian tapas) with top-notch house soave, or *pallottoline* (mini-bottles of beer) with generous *sopressa* (soft salami) *panini*. (☏041 523 95 77; Fondamenta Nani 992; ☺8.30am-8.30pm Mon-Sat; 🚤Zattere)

Café Noir CAFE, BAR

17 Map p56, C1

Shocking but true: sometimes even Venetians need a break from *spritz*, and crave a fortifying Guinness or minty mojito instead. Cosy Café Noir obliges at strictly fair prices – no drink costs over €6, service included, even when there's live music. (☏041 71 09 25; Calle dei Preti 3805; ☺7am-2am Mon-Fri, 5pm-2am Sat, 9am-2am Sun; 🚤San Tomà)

Tea Room Beatrice TEA ROOM

18 Map p56, B3

After long museum days, Beatrice offers a relaxing alternative to espresso bolted at a bar. Rainy days call for iron pots of green tea and almond cake, and sunshine brings iced drinks and salty pistachios to the garden patio. Gossip is a given in this discreet spot with Venice's best eavesdropping (overheard: 'But I'm old enough to be your grandmother...') (☏041 724 10 42; Calle Lunga San Barnaba 2727a; ☺3-10pm; 🚤Ca' Rezzonico)

Caffè Bar Ai Artisti CAFE, BAR

19 Map p56, C3

The cast of characters who sweep into this tiny cafe throughout the day seem borrowed from Pietro Longhi's paintings at neighbouring Ca' Rezzonico. Cheerful bartenders aren't the least fazed by dashing caped strangers swilling double espresso, or spaniels tucked underarm jealously eyeing the pastries. (☏393 968 01 35; Campo San Barnaba 2771; ☺7am-midnight Mon-Sat, from 9am Sun; 🚤Ca' Rezzonico)

 Local Life
Showtime at the Scuola

Music and dancing in a religious institution? Rome tried to forbid it for centuries, but the Venetian tradition continues today at the Scuola Grande dei Carmini (p59) with **Musica in Maschera** (Musical Masquerade; ☏347 912 24 50; www .musicainmaschera.it; tickets €20-50; ☺9pm Sep-Jul) concerts performed in 1700s costume with opera singers and a ballet corps. Tickets are available downstairs at the Scuola.

Entertainment

Venice Jazz Club
LIVE MUSIC

20 Map p56, C2

Jazz is alive and swinging in Dorsoduro, where the resident Venice Jazz Club Quartet pays regular respects to Miles Davis and John Coltrane, heats up on Latin Friday, and grooves to bossa nova and chanteuse standards. Drinks are steep, so starving artists booze beforehand and arrive by 8pm to pounce on complimentary cold-cut platters. (☏041 523 20 56; www.venicejazz-club.com; Ponte dei Pugni 3102; admission incl 1st drink €20; ☉doors 7pm, set begins 9pm, closed Aug; ⛴Ca' Rezzonico)

Shopping

Marina e Susanna Sent
ARTISANAL, GLASS

21 🔒 Map p56, E4

Wearable waterfalls and unpoppable bubble necklaces are Venice style signatures, thanks to the Murano-born Sent sisters, whose minimalist art-glass statement jewellery is featured in museum shops worldwide. See new collections at this flagship, their Murano studio, or the San Marco branch (at Ponte San Moise 2090). (☏041 520 81 36; www.marinaesusannasent.com; Campo San Vio 669; ☉10am-1pm & 3-6.30pm Tue-Sat, 3-6.30pm Mon; ⛴Accademia)

Danghyra
ARTISANAL, CERAMICS

22 🔒 Map p56, C2

Spare white bisque cups seem perfect for a Zen tea ceremony, but look inside: that iridescent lilac glaze is pure Carnevale. Danghyra's striking ceramics are hand-thrown in Venice with a magic touch – her platinum-glazed bowls make the simplest pasta dish appear fit for a modern doge. (☏041 522 41 95; www.danghyra.com; Calle delle Botteghe 3220; ☉10am-1pm & 3-7pm Tue-Sun; ⛴San Tomà)

Lauretta Vistosi
ARTISAN, ACCESSORIES

23 🔒 Map p56, C3

Murano-born artisan Lauretta Vistosi's signature, handmade handbags, eyeglass cases and journals are emblazoned with Murano-glass bulls-eyes. Each piece has flourishes like contrasting orange outstitching, and prices are surprisingly reasonable for one-of-a-kind finds, starting at €18. (☏041 528 65 30; www.laurettavistosi.org; Calle Lunga San Barnaba 2866b; ☉10am-1pm & 3-7pm Tue-Sat; ⛴Ca' Rezzonico)

Madera
DESIGN STORE

24 🔒 Map p56, C3

At this modern design showcase, iron cauldrons are reinvented as must-have kitchenware and sleek, gold tote bags are woven from reclaimed plastic bags. Owner-designer Francesca Meratti stocks a fine selection of Italian and Scandinavian designs that are original, portable and affordable, starting at

€14. (☑041 522 41 81; www.shopmaderav
ezia.it; Campo San Barnaba 2762; ⊙10am-1pm
& 4.30-7.30pm Tue-Sat; ☻Ca' Rezzonico)

L'Angolo del Passato
ANTIQUES, HOMEWARES

25 Map p56, D2

The 19th century bumps into the 21st
in this hidden corner showcase of rare
Murano glass, ranging from spun-gold
chandeliers to smoked-glass sconces.
Contemporary items line the back
shelves, including blown-glass vases
with graffiti-graphic squiggles. (☑041
528 78 96; Campiello dei Squelini 3276; ⊙10am-
1pm & 3-7pm Mon-Sat; ☻Ca' Rezzonico)

Papuni Art
ARTISANAL, JEWELLERY

26 Map p56, C3

Handmade, industrial chic isn't
expected across the footbridge from
baroque Ca' Rezzonico, but Venetian
artisan Ninfa Salerno delights in the
unexpected. Staid pearl strands are
given a sense of humour with bouncy
black rubber and Murano glass beads
are embedded in rubber daisy cocktail
rings. (☑041 241 04 34; www.papuniart
.it; Ponte dei Pugni 2834a; ⊙11am-1pm &
3-7pm Mon & Wed-Sat, 11am-1pm Tue; ☻Ca'
Rezzonico)

Aqua Altra
HOME & GARDEN

27 Map p56, B2

This volunteer-run, fair-trade co-op
sells single-origin drinking chocolate
from Sierra Leone growers' collec-
tives, anti-aging argan-nut oil from

Top Tip

Dorsoduro Walking Distances

Dorsoduro points into the lagoon
like a slightly dinged gondola prow,
and sites are spread out. Museums
are along the Grand Canal on the
east side, while boisterous bars
and upbeat eateries are clumped
around Campo Santa Margherita
and Campo San Barnaba to the
northwest. Don't wait too long for
your lunch break: many restaurants stop serving lunch around
2pm, and the best options are a
20-minute walk from the Guggenheim or Punta della Dogana.

Moroccan women's cooperatives, and
match-standard footballs made by a
Pakistani cooperative. (☑041 521 12 59;
www.aquaaltra.it; Campo Santa Margherita
2898; ⊙9.30am-12.30pm & 4-7.30pm Tue-
Sat, 4-7.30pm Mon; ☻Ca' Rezzonico)

Le Forcole di Saverio Pastor
ARTISAN

28 Map p56, G4

Saverio Pastor individually designs
forcole (wooden gondola oarlocks) to
match a gondolier's height, weight
and movement. They twist elegantly,
striking an easy balance on gondolas
and mantelpieces alike. (☑041 522 56
99; www.forcole.com; Fondamenta Soranzo
detta Fornace 341; ⊙8.30am-12.30pm &
2.30-6pm Mon-Sat; ☻Salute)

Explore

San Polo & Santa Croce

Heavenly devotion and earthly delights are neighbours in San Polo and Santa Croce, featuring divine art alongside the ancient red-light district, now home to artisans' studios and Rialto Market–fresh dining hotspots. Besides Titian's glowing Madonna at I Frari and turbulent Tintorettos at Scuola Grande di San Rocco, Grand Canal palace museums showcase fashion, video art and scientific oddities.

The Sights in a Day

Start the morning among masterpieces at **Scuola Grande di San Rocco** (p68), then bask in the glow of Titian's *Assunta* at **I Frari** (p71). Browse backstreet artisans' boutiques to the **Rialto Market** (p72), where glistening purple octopus and feathery red radicchio pose for culinary photoops. Hungry yet? Stop at **All'Arco** (p80) for Rialto-Market–inspired *cicheti* (Venetian tapas).

Runway-stomp through four centuries of avant-garde fashion at **Fondazione Prada** (p78) and **Palazzo Mocenigo** (p79), then swing by **Alaska** (p81) to celebrate freedom from corsetry with adventurous gelato. Make like Marco Polo and follow Venetian explorers' trails through a world of natural wonders at the **Museo di Storia Naturale** (p78).

Toast the splendours of nature with all-natural wines at **Al Prosecco** (p83). Wander the maze of Venice's former red-light district to **Antiche Carampane** (p80) for dinner, or get romantic with concerts at the frescoed pleasure palace of **Palazzetto Bru Zane** (p85).

For a local's day in San Polo, see p74.

Top Sights

Scuola Grande di San Rocco (p68)

I Frari (p71)

Rialto Market (p72)

Local Life

Fashion Finds (p74)

Best of Venice

Shopping

Cárte (p74)

Gilberto Penzo (p87)

Pied à Terre (p75)

I Vetri a Lume di Amadi (p88)

Cartavenezia (p88)

Eating

All'Arco (p80)

Antiche Carampane (p80)

Dai Zemei (p81)

Getting There

Vaporetto Most call at Piazzale Roma in Santa Croce. In San Polo, lines 1, 4 and N stop at Rialto. Line 1 also stops at Rialto–Mercato (daytime), Riva de Biasio, San Stae (line N too), San Silvestro and San Tomà (line N also).

Top Sights
Scuola Grande di San Rocco

You'll swear the paint is still fresh on the 50 action-packed, strikingly modern Tintorettos completed between 1575 and 1587 for the Scuola Grande di San Rocco, dedicated to the patron saint of the plague-stricken. While the 1575–77 plague claimed one-third of Venice's residents, Tintoretto painted nail-biting scenes of looming despair and last-minute redemption, illuminating a survivor's struggle with breathtaking urgency.

Map p76, B5

scuolagrandesanrocco.it

Campo San Rocco 3052, San Polo

adult €8, incl Scuola Grande dei Carmini €12

9.30am-5.30pm

San Tomà

Interior, Scuola Grande di San Rocco

Don't Miss

Sala Grande Superiore

Tintoretto's Old Testament ceiling scenes read like a modern comic: you can almost hear the 'swoop!' overhead as an angel dives down to feed ailing Elijah. Meanwhile, eerie illumination ominously strikes subjects in dark New Testament wall scenes. When Tintoretto painted these scenes, the plague had just taken 50,000 Venetians, and the cause and cure were unknown. With dynamic lines pointing to glimmers of hope on still-distant horizons, Tintoretto created a moving parable for epidemics through the ages.

Sala Albergo

Every surviving Venetian artist wanted the commission to paint the building dedicated to San Rocco (St Roch), patron saint of plague victims, so Tintoretto cheated. Instead of offering sketches like rival Paolo Veronese, Tintoretto dedicated a complete *tondo* (ceiling panel) to the saint, knowing such a gift couldn't be matched.

Tintoretto's newly restored *St Roch in Glory* is surrounded by representations of the four seasons and the saving graces of Felicity, Generosity, Faith and Hope. Feeble Hope is propped up on one elbow – still reeling from the tragedy of the plague, but miraculously alive.

Assembly Hall

Downstairs are works by other Venetian A-list artists, including Titian, Giorgione and Tiepolo. But Tintoretto steals the scene with the Virgin Mary's life story, starting on the left wall with *Annunciation,* where the angel surprises Mary at her sewing. The cycle ends with a dark, cataclysmic *Ascension,* unlike Titian's glowing version at I Frari.

☑ Top Tips

▶ Ask at the front counter about Assembly Hall Gregorian chant concerts – fitting soundracks to Tintoretto's haunting paintings.

▶ Grab a mirror to avoid neck strain as you see saints make heroic rescues in Tintoretto's ceiling panels.

▶ Through a side door upstairs lies the newly opened Tesoro (Treasury), containing a coral candelabra and 13th-century Iranian lustreware.

▶ A portrait of Tintoretto with his paintbrushes is captured in Francesco Pianta's recently restored 17th-century carved-wood sculpture. Look upstairs, third from the right beneath Tintoretto's New Testament masterpieces.

✗ Take a Break

Celebrate Venice's survival against the odds with dark chocolate plague-doctor masks at VizioVirtù (p88) or *prosecco* and *panini* at Caffè dei Frari (p84).

Top Sights
I Frari

Like moths to an eternal flame, visitors are inexorably drawn to the front of this dim, cavernous 14th-century cathedral by a tiny, luminous Titian altarpiece. Also known as Basilica di Santa Maria Gloriosa dei Frari, this church is a towering achievement, with intricate marquetry choir stalls, a rare Bellini and a creepy Longhena funeral monument. Italian Gothic I Frari omits flying buttresses, pinnacles and gargoyles in favour of small, striking details: contrasting red-and-white mouldings, high oculi (porthole windows) and delicate scalloping under the roofline.

⊙ Map p76, C5

www.chorusvenezia.org

Campo dei Frari 3004, San Polo

adult/reduced €3/1.50

⊙ 9am-6pm Mon-Sat, 1-6pm Sun

☐ San Tomà

Central nave. I Frari

Don't Miss

Titian Masterpieces

I Frari's crowning glory is Titian's 1518 *Assunta* (Ascension) altarpiece, showing a radiant Madonna stepping onto a cloud and escaping this mortal coil in a swirl of Titian-red robes. Both inside and outside the painting, onlookers gasp and point at the sight: with careful 2012 restoration by Save Venice, Titian's Madonna is positively glowing. According to local lore, the glimpse of the Madonna's luminous wrist has led monks to recant their chastity vows.

Titian upstaged his own 1526 Pesaro altarpiece, a dreamlike composite family portrait of the Holy Family with the Venetian Pesaro family. The great painter was lost to the plague at 90 in 1576, but legend has it that in light of his masterpieces, Venice's strict rules of quarantine were bent to allow Titian's burial inside I Frari.

Side Altars

I Frari's other Madonna masterpiece is in the sacristy: Bellini's achingly sweet and startlingly 3D *Madonna with Child* triptych. The Capella Corner honours Venice's patron saint in Bartolomeo's *St Mark Enthroned*, showing the fluffy-bearded saint serenaded by an angelic orchestra.

Monuments

Setting the stage for Titian's masterpiece is the magnificent marquetry *coro* (choir stall), with architectural puzzlework details worthy of MC Escher. Baldassare Longhena's eerie Doge Pesaro funereal monument is hoisted by four burly, black-marble figures. Disconsolate mourners dab at their eyes with the hems of their cloaks on Canova's marble pyramid mausoleum, originally intended as a monument to Titian.

☑ **Top Tips**

▶ No phones, cameras or food are allowed in the church, and appropriate dress (eg no shorts, miniskirts, midriff- or tank-tops) is required. Note that last admittance is 5.30pm.

▶ Tolling bells give fair warning when the church closes for mass. The *campanile* (bell tower) has remained upright and active since 1386 – a rare feat, given Venice's shifting *barene* (shoals).

✕ **Take a Break**

Emerge from Gothic gloom into broad sunlight for seafood pasta in the garden at Trattoria da Ignazio (p82) or pizza in Campo San Polo at Birraria La Corte (p82).

Top Sights
Rialto Market

Venice has its priorities straight: before you conquer the world, you gotta eat. Before there was a bridge at the Rialto or palaces lining the Grand Canal, Venice established its Pescaria (fish market) and Rialto produce market. Restaurants worldwide are catching on to a secret that Venice's market vendors have loudly touted for 700 years: food tastes better when it's fresh, seasonal and local.

👁 Map p76, H3

📞 041 296 06 58

🕐 7am-2pm, Pescaria closed Mon

🚤 Rialto-Mercato

Fish, Rialto Market

Don't Miss

Ponte di Rialto

An amazing feat of engineering in its day, Antonio da Ponte's 1592 marble bridge was for centuries the only land link across the Grand Canal. It cost 250,000 gold ducats (about €19 million today) – a staggering sum that puts cost overruns for the new Ponte di Calatrava into perspective. After the crowds of shutterbugs and tour groups clear out around sunset, the southern side facing San Marco offers panoramas of a picturesque stretch of the Grand Canal lined with gondolas and *palazzi* (palaces).

Pescaria

Slinging fresh fish for seven centuries and still going strong, the Pescaria's fishmongers are more vital to Venetian cuisine than any chef. Starting at 7am, they sing the praises of today's catch: mountains of glistening *moscardini* (baby octopus), icebergs of inky *seppie* (cuttlefish) and buckets of crabs, from tiny *moeche* (soft-shell crabs) to *granseole* (spider crabs).

The Pescaria was rebuilt in 1907, after constant use had left the earlier structure salt-corroded. Sustainable fishing practices are not new here: marble plaques show regulations set centuries ago for minimum allowable sizes for lagoon fish.

Produce Market

Compared with tame supermarket specimens, Veneto veggies look like they landed from another planet. Tiny purplish Sant'Erasmo *castraure* (baby artichokes) look like alien heads, white Bassano asparagus seems to have sprouted on the moon, and red radicchio could be mutant Martian flowers.

☑ **Top Tips**

▶ Sunset gondola rides under the Ponte di Rialto (Rialto bridge) are romantic, but run €100 per 40-minute minimum after 7pm. For cheap daytime thrills, hop the Rialto Mercato *traghetto* (public gondola) and cross the Grand Canal standing for just €1.50.

▶ Note the line-caught lagoon seafood available at the Pescaria, and you'll recognise tasty, sustainable options on dinner menus.

▶ To avoid crowded kiosks and foot-traffic jams on the Ponte di Rialto, do what locals do: zip up the less scenic northern side of the bridge.

✗ **Take a Break**

Join Pescaria fisherman at the All'Arco (p80) counter for *cicheti* inspired daily by the Rialto Market's best finds. For picnics by the Rialto docks, get seafood salads and pasta to go at ProntoPesce (p81).

Local Life
Fashion Finds

Treasure-hunt through San Polo artisan studios and design boutiques, and find your own signature Venetian style to stand out in any opening-night crowd. From one-of-a-kind paper jewels to custom velvet slippers, Venice's most original fashion statements ensure no one can steal your look – and usually cost less than global brands.

❶ Paper Jewels at Cárte

Lagoon ripples swirl across marbled-paper statement necklaces and hypnotic handbags, thanks to the steady hands and restless imagination of *carta marmorizzata* (marbled-paper) maestra Rosanna Corrò at **Cárte** (☏320 024 87 76; www.cartevenezia .it; Calle dei Cristi 1731, San Polo; ⓧ11am-5pm Mon-Sat, to 3pm Nov-Mar; ☝Rialto-Mercato). After years restoring ancient Venetian books, Corrò began creating her origi-

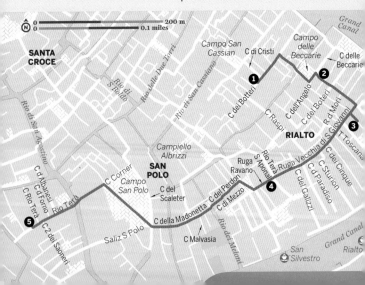

nal, bookish beauties: aquatic cocktail rings, op-art brooches and zig-zagged jewellery boxes. Wall panels, wedding albums and even chairs can be custom ordered.

❷ Fierce Clutches at Il Gufo Artigiano

Hot copper and extremely careful handling are the secrets to the embossed leather designs gracing totes, clutches and wallets in this artisan's **atelier** (☑041 523 40 30; Ruga degli Speziali 299, San Polo; ☉10am-3.30pm Mon-Sat; ☴Rialto-Mercato). Ancient ironwork patterns in Venetian windows inspire the swirling designs on saffron albums and green journals, while the winged lion of St Mark roars with high-fashion fierceness on scarlet handbags and tawny satchels.

❸ Furlane Shoes at Pied à Terre

Rialto courtesans and their 30cm-high heels are long gone, but Venetian slippers stay stylish. Colourful *furlane* (slippers) are handcrafted at **Pied à Terre** (☑041 528 55 13; www .piedaterre-venice.com; Sotoportego degli Oresi 60, San Polo; ☉10am-1pm & 3-7pm Tue-Sat, 3-7pm Mon; ☴Rialto) with recycled bicycle-tyre treads, ideal for finding your footing on a gondola. Choose from velvet, brocade or raw silk in vibrant shades of lemon and ruby, with optional piping. Don't see your size? Shoes can be custom-made and shipped.

❹ Artistic Attire at Hibiscus

Blend in at the Biennale with Venice's creative crossroads style, layered piece by distinctive piece at **Hibiscus** (☑041 520 89 89; Ruga Ravano 1061, San Polo; ☉10am-7.30pm; ☴San Silvestro). Think easygoing Italian linen swing dresses, Okinawan indigo wrap jackets, violet Kashmiri cashmere shawls, French watercolour-patterned socks and Maria Calderara pop-art resin necklaces. More original than most ready-to-wear and priced accordingly, but sales are fabulous.

❺ Runway Wraps at Anatema

Add a Venetian eye for colour to a Japanese flair for sculptural fashion, and here you have it: teal Italian mohair tube scarves that float around the collarbone like clouds, and pleated Thai silk shawls in neon-yellow shades worthy of Milan runways. Venetian-Japanese design duo **Anatema** (☑041 524 22 21; www.anatema. it; Rio Terà 2603, San Polo; ☉10am-2pm & 3-7pm; ☴San Tomà) brings out new collections each season, from sunhats to wool-felt brooches.

A **B** **C** **D**

1

Grand Canal

Fond dei Scalzi

Riva de Biasio

Riva di Biasio

C Zen

Campo Riello

Campo San Giovanni Decollato

Museo di Storia Natura di Venezia
2

Ponte dei Scalzi

C del Pistor

C Pisani

Rio Terà

Salizz del Fondaco dei Turchi

Rio di San Zan Degolà

Ferrovia Scalzi

C Lunga Chioverette

Rio Marin

Lista dei Bari
9

C Gallion

C Orsetti

Salizz Zusto

Rio Terà

Rio Terà dell'Isola

C dell'Isola

12

Tent

C Colombo

2

Cllo de Comare

Cllo di Comare

SANTA CROCE

C d Croce

C Larga dei Bari

Fond Rio Marin o Garzotti

C d Croce

Campo San Nazario Sauro

Ramo Cazza

C del Savio

C di Ruga Vecchia dell'Orio

Chiesa di San Giacomo dell'Orio
5

Campo San Giacomo dell'Orio

Larga

C Zambelli

17

C Bergamaschi

C Chioverette

F Gradenigo

Fond Rio Marin o Garzotti

C Gradisca

Ruga Bella

C Larga

C del Tentor
19

C S Boldo

36

35

3

Campo della Lana

Corte Canal

C Viscigia

C Larga Contarina

Rio di San Zuane

C San Zuane

C dell'Olio

C delle Oche

C Cappello

Rio di San Cristo

C di Chiesa

C della Lana

C della Lacca

Campiello della Scuola

25

24

C Zane

C della Vida

C d Chiesa

Rio di San Agostin

4

Corte di Amai

C Campazzo

C delle Chiovere

C Dro l'Archivio

Rio Terà San Tomà

Campo San Stin

C Dona

Fond Contarini

Rio di San Polo

C Larg

Ramo Cimesin

Rio delle Succhere

SAN POLO

C Rio Terà

C d'Albanesi

C d Forno

Rio Terà
30

C Faller

C del Forno

C Molini

C Tintoretto

Campo dei Frari

20

Fond dei Frari

Salizz San Rocco

C z de C Moro

C del Saoner

27

5

Saliz San Pantalon

C Vinanti

Scuola Grande di San Rocco

I Frari

Campo San Rocco

C dei Corte

Rio di San Tomà

15

31

C dei Nomboli

Rio del Malcanton

Campiello Mosca

C della Scuola

C dei Scaleter

C Crosera

C Gozzi

C d Cristo

Campo San Tomà

32

C del Campaniel

C Traghetto

For reviews see

◉	Top Sights	p68
◉	Sights	p78
✖	Eating	p80
🍷	Drinking	p83
★	Entertainment	p85
🛍	Shopping	p87

N
0 — 200 m
0 — 0.1 miles

Rio Fontego del Turchi

C del Meggio

Rio di Noale

Campo San Felice

San Stae

Campo San Stae

Saliz di San Stae

C del Forno

Fond Rimpetto Mocenigo

Rio di San Felice

Ca' Pesaro

1

Fondazione Prada

3

CANNAREGIO

Rio di Noale

C Carminati

4

Palazzo Mocenigo

C delle Grue

C d Chiesa

C del Tozzo

C del Ravano

Rio delle Due Torri

C Corner

C della Rosa

Grand Canal

Ca' d'Oro

Campo Santa Sofia

Strada Nuova

C Miani

Ca' d'Oro Traghetto

Ca' d'Oro Traghetto

Campo della Pescaria

C del Carampanei

Fond dell'Olio

Sotoportego de siora Bettina

Rio di San Cassiano

C del Botter

Rialto Market

28

29

Rio della Pergola

C Lunga

Campo Santa Maria Mater Domini

C dell'Agnello

C del Cristo

C Filosi

C dei Muti o Baglioni

Ponte delle Tette

8

Rio dei Meloni

C Albrizzi

Campiello Albrizzi

Rio di San Cassiano

C dell'Angelo

Rio dei Beccarie

C delle Beccarie

10

Rialto-Mercato

R dei Morti

21

Ruga dei Oresi

23

18

Campo San Giacometto

6

33

C Galeazza

Saliz dei do Mori

C dell'Arco

22

Ruga Vecchia di San Giovanni

Chiesa di San Giovanni Elemosinario

11

Rio Terà delle Carampane

Calle delle Do Spade

C Raspi

RIALTO

13

C dei Cinque

16

C Scaleter

Rio dei Melora

14

C del Scaleter

C dei Cavalli

26

Campo San Polo

C della Madonetta

C del Perdon

Ruga Ravano

Campo S Silvestro

C Dolera

C dei Paradiso

C d Sturion

C dei Galizzi

Campo San Bartolomeo

C Larga Mazzini

Riz S Polo

C d Magazen

C della Madonnetta

Rio della Madonnetta

San Silvestro

C Tiepolo

Grand Canal

Fond del Vin

Rialto

Riva del Carbon

C Bembo

Corte del Teatro

C del Carbon

C dei Loredan

C Cavalli

Rio di San Silvador

C del l'Ovo

SAN MARCO

Sights

Ca' Pesaro
MUSEUM

1 Map p76, F2

Like a Carnevale costume built for two, the stately exterior of this Baldassare Longhena–designed 1710 *palazzo* hides two quirky museums: **Galleria Internazionale d'Arte Moderna** and **Museo d'Arte Orientale**. Galleria d'Arte Moderna covers three floors and highlights Venice's role in modern-art history, while the attic holds treasures from Prince Enrico di Borbone's epic 1887–89 souvenir-shopping spree across Asia. (Galleria Internazionale d'Arte Moderna e Museo d'Arte Orientale; ☎041 72 11 27; www.visitmuve.it; Fondamenta di Ca' Pesaro 2070, Santa Croce; adult/reduced €8/5.50, or with Museum Pass; ⏰10am-6pm Tue-Sun Apr-Oct, to 5pm Nov-Mar; 🚤San Stae)

Understand
Venice's Saving Graces

While the Black Death ravaged the rest of Europe, Venice mounted an interfaith effort against the plague. The city dedicated a church and *scuola* (religious confraternity) to San Rocco where Venetians could pray for deliverance from the disease, while also consulting resident Jewish and Muslim doctors about prevention measures. Venice established the world's first quarantine zone, with inspections and 40-day waiting periods for incoming ships at Lazaretto. Venice's forward-thinking, inclusive approach created Scuola Grande di San Rocco's artistic masterpieces, which provide comfort to the afflicted and bereaved to this day, and set a public-health standard that has saved countless lives down the centuries.

Museo di Storia Naturale di Venezia
MUSEUM

2 Map p76, D1

Venice's wildest adventure begins with dinosaurs, then dashes through evolution and enters Venice's age of exploration, when adventurers like Marco Polo fetched scientific marvels from distant lands. Pass mummies and enter a *wunderkammer* (curiosity cabinet) covered with shark jaws and poisonous blowfish. Adorning the exit staircase are heraldic symbols of kissing doves, marking the building's history as a ducal palace and Turkish trading house. (Fondaco dei Turchi; ☎041 275 02 06; http://msn.visitmuve.it; Salizada del Fontego dei Turchi 1730, Santa Croce; adult/reduced €8/5.50, or with Museum Pass; ⏰10am-6pm Tue-Sun, to 5pm Tue-Fri Nov-May; 🚤San Stae)

Fondazione Prada
MUSEUM

3 Map p76, F2

This stately Grand Canal palace has been commandeered by Fondazione Prada, but you won't necessarily find handbags here. Instead Ca' Corner

Ca' Pesaro

showcases the art and avant-garde design that have shaped modern visual sensibilities, from Fortunato Depero's fragmented Futurist suits to Andy Warhol's Brillo boxes. Rotating multimedia shows are imaginative and exhaustive, though one visiting dachshund critic yawned audibly at early video art. (Ca' Corner; ☑041 810 91 61; www.fondazioneprada.org; Calle de Ca' Corner 2215, Santa Croce; adult/reduced €10/ free; ☺10am-6pm Wed-Mon during exhibitions; ☣San Stae)

Palazzo Mocenigo

MUSEUM

4 ◉ Map p76, E2

Hello, gorgeous: from 18th-century duchess *andrienne* (hip-extending dresses) to Anne Hathaway's mega-ruffled Versace Venice Film Festival ballgown, Palazzo Mocenigo's historic, head-turning fashion will leave you feeling glamorous by association, if a tad underdressed. Necklines plunge in the **Red Living Room**, lethal corsets come undone in the **Contessa's Bedroom** and men's paisley knee-breeches reveal leg in the **Dining Room**. (☑041 72 17 98; http://mocenigo.visitmuve.it; Salizada di San Stae 1992, Santa Croce; adult/ reduced €5/3.50, or with Museum Pass; ☺10am-5pm Tue-Sun Apr-Oct, to 4pm Nov-Mar; ☣San Stae)

Chiesa di San Giacomo dell'Orio
CHURCH

5 Map p76, D2

La Serenissima seems serene as ever inside the cool gloom of this Romanesque church, founded in the 9th to 10th centuries and completed in Latin-cross form by 1225, with chapels bubbling along the edges. Notable 14th- to 18th-century artworks include luminous sacristy paintings by Palma Il Giovane, a rare Lorenzo Lotto *Madonna with Child and Saints* and an exceptional Veronese crucifix (currently undergoing restoration). (www.chorusvenezia.org; Campo San Giacomo dell'Orio 1457, Santa Croce; admission €3, or with Chorus Pass; ⏰10am-5pm Mon-Sat; 🚤Riva de Biasio)

Chiesa di San Giovanni Elemosinario
CHURCH

6 Map p76, H3

Hunkering modestly behind skimpy T-shirt kiosks is this soaring Renaissance brick church, built by Scarpagnino after a disastrous fire in 1514 destroyed much of the Rialto area. Cross the darkened threshhold to witness flashes of Renaissance genius: Titian's tender *St John the Almsgiver* (freshly restored and returned from the Accademia) and gloriously restored dome frescoes of frolicking angels by Pordenone. (Ruga Vecchia di San Giovanni 477, San Polo; admission €3, or with Chorus Pass; ⏰10am-5pm Mon-Sat, 1-5pm Sun; 🚤Rialto-Mercato)

Eating

All'Arco
VENETIAN $

7 Map p76, G3

Father-son *maestri* Francesco and Matteo invent Venice's best *cicheti* daily with Rialto Market finds. Behind marble counters, Francesco wraps poached Bassano white asparagus with seasoned pancetta, while Matteo creates *otrega* (butterfish) *crudo* (Venetian-style sushi) with mint–olive oil marinade and Hawaiian red-clay salt. Be patient: even with copious *prosecco* (Venetian sparkling wine), hardly any meal here tops €20 or falls short of five stars. (☑041 520 56 66; Calle dell'Ochialer 436; cicheti €1.50-4; ⏰8am-3.30pm Mon-Sat, plus 6-9pm Apr-Oct, closed Jul & Aug; 🚤Rialto-Mercato)

Antiche Carampane
VENETIAN $$

8 Map p76, F3

Hidden in the lanes behind Ponte delle Tette, this culinary indulgence is a trick to find. The sign proudly announcing 'no tourist menu' signals a welcome change: say goodbye to soggy lasagne and hello to silky, lagoon-fresh *crudi*, asparagus and *granseola* (lagoon crab) salad, cloudlike gnocchi, and San Pietro (whitefish) atop grilled radicchio. (☑041 524 01 65; www.antichecarampane.com; Rio Terà delle Carampane 1911, San Polo; meals €30-45; ⏰noon-2.30pm & 7-11pm Tue-Sat; 🚤San Stae)

Alaska Gelateria   GELATO $

9 ✕ Map p76, B2

Outlandish organic artisanal gelato: enjoy a Slow Food scoop of house-roasted local pistachio, or two of the tangy Sicilian lemon with vaguely minty Sant'Erasmo *carciofi* (artichokes). Even vegans are spoiled for choice of flavours, including watermelon and rose. Kids who choose strawberry *granita* (shaved ice) can top the confection with a leaf plucked from the basil plant on the counter. (☑041 71 52 11; Calle Larga dei Bari 1159, Santa Croce; gelati €1-2; ⏱noon-8pm; 👶; ⛴Riva de Biasio)

ProntoPesce   SEAFOOD, CICHETI $

10 ✕ Map p76, G3

Alongside Venice's fish market, this designer deli serves artfully composed *crudi*, well-dressed seafood salads, legendary Saturday-only fish risotto (served at 1pm exactly) and superb shellfish stews in winter. Grab a stool and an (unfortunately) plastic glass of DOC soave with *folpetti* (baby octopus) salad and plump prawn *crudi,* or enjoy yours dockside along the Grand Canal. (☑041 822 02 98; www.prontopesce .it; Rialto Pescheria 319, San Polo; cicheti €3-8; ⏱9am-2.45pm & 7-11.30pm Tue-Sat; ⛴Rialto-Mercato)

Al Pesador   MODERN ITALIAN $$$

11 ✕ Map p76, H3

Watch the world drift down the Grand Canal outside or canoodle indoors, but prepare to sit up and pay attention once the food arrives. Pesador reinvents Venetian cuisine with culinary finesse: *cicheti* feature mackerel with *saor* (balsamic-vinegar marinade) and paper-thin *lardo crostini* (cured pork fat on toast) with mint oil, while *primi* (mains) include red-footed scallops kicking wild herbs across squid-ink gnocchi. (☑041 523 94 92; www.alpesador .it; Campo San Giacometto 125, San Polo; cicheti €1.50-5, meals €40-55; ⏱noon-3pm & 7-11pm Mon-Sat; ⛴Rialto-Mercato)

Osteria La Zucca   MODERN ITALIAN $$

12 ✕ Map p76, D2

Vegetable-centric, seasonal small plates bring Venetian spice-trade influences to local produce: zucchini with ginger zing, cinnamon-tinged pumpkin flan, and raspberry spice cake. Herbed roast lamb is respectable here too, but the island-grown produce is the breakout star. The snug wood-panelled interior gets toasty, so reserve canalside seats in summer. (☑041 524 15 70; www.lazucca.it; Calle del Tintor 1762, Santa Croce; meals €30-45; ⏱12.30-2.30pm & 7-10.30pm Mon-Sat; ⏷; ⛴San Stae)

Dai Zemei   VENETIAN, CICHETI $

13 ✕ Map p76, G4

The *zemei* (twins) who run this closet-sized *cicheti* counter serve loyal regulars and well-informed foodie tourists small meals with outsized imagination: octopus salad with marinated rocket, duck breast drizzled

CUBOIMAGES SRL / ALAMY ©

Crab salad, Antiche Carampane (p80)

with truffle oil, or *crostini* loaded with tuna-leek salad. It's a gourmet bargain for inspired bites and DOC/IGT wine pairings – try floral Ribolla Gialla or sophisticated Valpolicella. (☑041 520 85 46; www.ostariadaizemei.it; Ruga Vecchia San Giovanni 1045, San Polo; cicheti €1.50-4; ☺9am-8pm Wed-Mon; ☲San Silvestro)

Birraria La Corte
PIZZERIA, RISTORANTE $$

 14 Map p76, E4

This former bullfight pen became a brewery in the 19th century to keep Venice's Austrian occupiers occupied, and beer and heritage beef remain reliable bets here. Perennial favourites include *bresaola* (air-cured beef) and rocket and buffalo-mozzarella pizzas,

with German beer on tap or Italian artisan bottled brews. There's seldom a wait for indoor seating, though piazza seating is prime in summer. (☑041 275 05 70; www.birrarialacorte.it; Campo San Polo 2168; pizzas €8-13, mains €15; ☲San Silvestro)

Trattoria da Ignazio
VENETIAN, SEAFOOD $$

 15 Map p76, D5

Dapper, white-jacketed waiters serve pristine grilled lagoon fish, fresh pasta and desserts made in-house ('of course') with a proud flourish on tables bedecked with yellow linens and orchids. On cloudy days, home-made crab pasta with a bright Lugana white wine make a fine substitute for sunshine. On sunny days and warm nights, the neighbourhood converges beneath the garden's grape arbour. (☑041 523 48 52; www.trattoriadaignazio .com; Calle dei Saoneri 2749, San Polo; meals €25-30; ☺noon-3pm & 7-11pm Mon-Sat; ⧉; ☻San Tomà)

Sacro E Profano ITALIAN $

16 Map p76, H4

Musicians, artists and philosophising regulars make this hideaway under the Rialto exceptionally good for eavesdropping – but once that hand-made gnocchi or spaghetti *alla búsara* (Venetian prawn sauce) arrives, all talk is reduced to satisfied mur-murs. The place is run by a Venetian ska-band leader, which explains the trumpets on the wall and the upbeat, arty scene. (☑041 523 79 24; Ramo Terzo del Parangon 502, San Polo; meals €15-25; ☺11.30am-1pm & 6.30pm-1am Mon-Tue & Thu-Sat, 11.30am-2pm Sun; ☻Rialto-Mercato)

Drinking

Al Prosecco WINE BAR

17 Map p76, D2

The urge to toast sunsets in Venice's loveliest *campo* is only natural – and so is the wine at Al Prosecco. This forward-thinking bar specialises in *vini naturi* (natural-process wines) – organic, biodynamic, wild yeast fermented – from the €3.50 unfiltered 'cloudy' *prosecco* to the silky €5 Veneto Venegazzù that trails across

the tongue and lingers in the imagina-tion. (☑041 524 02 22; www.alprosecco .com; Campo San Giacomo dell'Orio, Santa Croce 1503; ☺9am-10.30pm Mon-Sat, to 8pm winter; ☻San Stae)

Al Mercà WINE BAR

18 Map p76, H3

Discerning drinkers throng this cupboard-sized bar crammed with *cicheti* and 60 different wines, includ-ing top-notch *prosecco* and DOC wines by the glass (€2 to €3.50). Arrive by 6.30pm for meatballs and mini-*panini*

Understand
Ponte delle Tette

No one remembers the original name of **Ponte delle Tette** (Map p76, F3; ☻San Silvestro), known since the 15th century as 'Tits Bridge'. Across this bridge was once Venice's red-light zone, where prostitutes displayed their wares in windows. But the most ambi-tious working girls might be found studying: for educated conversa-tion, *cortigiane* (courtesans) might charge 60 times the going rates for basic services. Fees set by the state were posted in brothels (soap cost extra), Venetian guide books published reviews of high-end *cortigiane*, and prostitutes were officially forbidden from cross-dressing (aka false advertising) or riding in two-oared boats – lucky that gondolas only require one oar.

(sandwiches; €1 to €2) and easy bar access, or mingle with crowds stretching to the Grand Canal docks – there's no seating, and it's elbow room only at Venice's friendliest bar counter. (☑393 992 47 81; Campo Cesare Battisti 213, San Polo; ⊙9.30am-2.30pm & 6-9pm Mon-Sat; 🛳Rialto)

Osteria da Filo CAFE, BAR

19 Map p76, D3

A living room where drinks are served, Hosteria alla Poppa comes complete with creaky sofas, free wi-fi, abandoned novels and board games for marathon sessions mastering the Italian version of *Risk*. Service is brusque, but drinks are cheap and Mediterranean tapas tasty. Wednesday is live-music night starting around 8pm – usually it's jazz, with the owner on the drums. (Hosteria alla Poppa; ☑041 524 65 54; Calle delle Oche, Santa Croce; ⊙11am-midnight Wed-Sun, from 5pm Mon & Tue; 🛜; 🛳Riva de Biasio)

Caffè dei Frari CAFE, BAR

20 Map p76, C4

Take your espresso with a heap of history at this century-old, carved wooden bar, or recover from the sensory overload of I Frari with a sandwich, a glass of wine and easy conversation at the dinky indoor cafe tables downstairs or on the Liberty-style wrought-iron balcony upstairs. (☑041 524 18 77; Fondamenta dei Frari 2564, San Polo; ⊙8am-9pm Mon-Sat; 🛳San Tomà)

Muro Vino e Cucina BAR

21 Map p76, H3

No velvet rope here, though it's the kind of buzzing, urban-chic place at which you'd expect to find one. The throng at Muro's sleek aluminum *cicheti* counter are on to something – no one wants to miss *sopressa* with porcini mushroom cream, or smoked goose and arugula *crostini*. Prices are friendly too, with wines by the glass starting at €2 and *cicheti* from €1.50 to €3.50. (☑041 241 23 39; www.murovenezia.com; Campo Bello Vienna 222, San Polo; ⊙9am-3pm & 5pm-2am Mon-Sat; 🛳Rialto)

Cantina Do Spade PUB

22 Map p76, G3

Since 1488 this bar has kept Venice in good spirits, and the laid-back young management extends warm welcomes to *spritz*-sipping Venetian regulars and visiting connoisseurs drinking double-malt Dolomite beer and bargain Venetian DOC cab franc. Come early for market-fresh *fritture* (batter-fried seafood; €2 to €6). (☑041 521 05 83; www.cantinadospade.it; Calle delle Do Spade 860, San Polo; ⊙10am-3pm & 6-10pm; 🛳Rialto)

Barcollo BAR

23 Map p76, H3

Consider permission to get happy granted: *barcollo* means stagger. DJs and sass from the handlebar-mustachioed bartender put the crowd in a party mood, especially on Wednesday buffet nights that draw university students by the dozen. Prices aren't staggering – an *ombra* (short glass) of DOC wine plus snacks of *polpette* (meatballs) runs under €5. (☎041 522 81 58; Campo Cesare Battista 219, San Polo; ☺5pm-midnight; ☻Rialto)

Entertainment

Palazzetto Bru Zane CLASSICAL MUSIC

24 ⭐ Map p76, C3

Pleasure palaces don't get more romantic than Palazzetto Bru Zane on concert nights, when exquisite harmonies tickle Sebastiano Ricci angels tumbling across stucco-frosted ceilings. Multiyear restorations have returned the 1695–97 Casino Zane's 100-seat music room to its original function, attracting world-class musicians to enjoy its acoustics. (Centre du Musique Romantique Française; ☎041 521 10 05; www.bru-zane.com; Palazzetto Bru Zane 2368, San Polo; adult/reduced €25/15; ☺box office 2.30-5.30pm Mon-Fri; ☻San Tomà)

Opera at Scuola Grande di San Giovanni Evangelista OPERA

25 ⭐ Map p76, C3

Drama comes with the scenery when Italian opera favourites – Puccini's *Tosca*, Verdi's *La Traviata*, Rossini's *Il Barbiere di Seviglia* – are performed in the lavish hall where Venice's secretive Council of Ten socialised. Stage sets can't compare to the Scuola:

Local Life
Tea in a Lagoon of Espresso

Espresso is everywhere in Venice, but Marco Polos with a taste for the finest teas from China seek out charming, art-filled **Tearoom Caffè Orientale** (Map p76, B2; ☎041 520 17 89; Rio Marin 888, Santa Croce; meals €6-12; ☺noon-9pm Fri-Wed). Baked goods are made in-house with extra-fluffy, high-protein Italian '00' flour – so after that whisper-light apple crumble or asparagus quiche, you'll be raring to tackle the museums.

sweep up Mauro Codussi's 15th-century staircase into Giorgio Massari's 1729 hall, and take your seat amid Giandomenico Tiepolo paintings. (☎041 426 65 59; www.scuolasangiovanni.it; Campiello della Scuola 2454, Santa Croce; adult/reduced from €30/25; ☺concerts 8.30pm; ☻San Tomà)

Arena di Campo San Polo CINEMA

26 ⭐ Map p76, E4

Where bullfights were once held by rowdy Austrians, the city now hosts free open-air films, and concerts and theatre performances in July and September – but watch this space year-round for kiddie carousels, political rallies and street musicians. (www.comune.venezia.it; Campo San Polo; ☺Jul & Aug; ☻San Silvestro)

Understand

The Grand Canal & its Bridges

Never was a thoroughfare so aptly named as the Grand Canal, reflecting the glories of Venetian architecture lining its banks. For maximum romance, drift down the Grand Canal by night, when dock lights turn into frenzied Tintoretto brush strokes in the water. Even public transport seems glamorous on the 3.5km *vaporetto* No 1 route, which follows the Grand Canal past some 50 *palazzi,* six churches and scene-stealing backdrops for four James Bond films.

Ponte Calatrava

Controversial Ponte di Calatrava is an ultramodern fish fin–shaped, glass-and-steel bridge by Spanish architect Santiago Calatrava that cost triple the original €4 million estimate. The 2008 bridge officially known as Ponte della Costituzione (Constitution Bridge) is the first to be built over the Grand Canal in 75 years.

Ponte degli Scalzi

The 'bridge of the barefoot' takes its name from the barefoot monks who used to pray at the nearby church. The stone bridge was designed by Eugenio Miozzi in 1934 to replace an iron bridge erected in 1875.

Ponte di Rialto

Construction costs for Antonio da Ponte's Ponte di Rialto spiralled to 250,000 Venetian ducats – about €19 million today. Legend has it that only a deal with the Devil allowed da Ponte to finish by 1592, yet this white Istrian stone bridge has remained a diabolically clever engineering feat – until chunks of bridge pylons dropped into the Grand Canal in 2011. Fashion company Diesel recently won a €5 million restoration bid, which may include advertising banners on construction scaffolding – prompting protest banners reading 'Our Town Is Not Bennetown'.

Ponte dell'Accademia

Wooden Ponte dell'Accademia was built in 1933 as a temporary replacement for an 1854 iron bridge, but this span arched like a cat's back remains a beloved landmark. Recent structural improvements have preserved this elegant little footbridge for decades to come.

Ponte dell'Accademia

Shopping

Gilberto Penzo ARTISANAL, BOATS

27 Map p76, D5

Yes, you actually can take a gondola home in your pocket. Anyone fascinated by the models at Museo Storico Navale will go wild here, amid handmade wooden models of all kinds of Venetian boats, including some that are seaworthy (or at least bathtub worthy). Signor Penzo also creates kits so crafty types and kids can have a crack at it themselves. (📞041 71 93 72; www.veniceboats.com; Calle 2 dei Saoneri 2681, San Polo; ⏰9am-12.30pm & 3-6pm Mon-Sat; 🚶; ⛴San Tomà)

Schantalle Vetri d'Arte ARTISANAL, GLASS

28 Map p76, E2

Murano must be jealous: Santa Croce boasts the new studio-showroom of glass-making power couple Schantalle Menegus and Igor Balbi. Homes become castles with Balbi's gossamer dragon goblets, poised for flight before you even finish your magic potion. Christmas arrives in Venice when Menegus twists Babbo Natale (Father Christmas) off her torch, Santa hat pulled low and nose rosy from *spritz*. (📞041 522 61 00; Campo Santa Maria Mater Domini 2115, Santa Croce; ⏰9am-12.30pm & 2-7pm Mon-Sat; ⛴San Stae)

Alberto Sarria Masks

Cartavenezia
ARTISANAL, PAPER

29 Map p76, E3

Paper is anything but two-dimensional here: paper maestro Fernando di Masone embosses and sculpts handmade cotton paper into seamless raw-edged lampshades, hand-bound sketchbooks and paper versions of marble friezes that would seem equally at home in a Greek temple or a modern loft. White gloves are handy for easy, worry-free browsing; paper-sculpting courses are available by prior request. (☑041 524 12 83; www.cartavenezia.it; Calle Lunga 2125, Santa Croce; ◷11am-1pm & 3.30-7.30pm Tue-Sat, 3.30-7.30pm Mon; ⚓San Stae)

Dietro L'Angolo
DESIGN STORE

30 Map p76, D4

Find modern Italian designs on a backstreet behind I Frari, with affordable, original pieces by young local and international designers. Blue pigeon earrings bring back San Marco memories, charming rat puppets support a local shelter, and herringbone-tweed cocktail rings with Murano-glass centres remind you it's time for a *spritz*. (☑041 524 30 71; www.dietrolangolo2657.com; Calle Seconda dei Saoneri 2657, San Polo; ⚓San Tomà)

I Vetri a Lume di Amadi
ARTISANAL, GLASS

31 Map p76, D5

Glass menageries don't get more fascinating than the one created before your eyes by Signor Amadi. Fierce little glass crabs approach pink-tipped sea anemones, and glass peas spill from a speckled pea pod. You might be tempted to swat at eerily lifelike glass mosquitoes, and the outlines of galloping horses in blue glass would do Picasso proud. (☑041 523 80 89; Calle Saoneri 2747, San Polo; ◷9am-12.30pm & 3-6pm Mon-Sat; ⚓San Tomà)

VizioVirtù
ARTISANAL, CHOCOLATE

32 Map p76, C5

Work your way through Venice's most decadent vices and tasty virtues at this Willy Wonka–esque chocolatier, from the hot-chocolate fountain to the dark-chocolate plague-doctor's masks.

Ganache-filled chocolates come in a five-course meal of flavours: barolo wine, pink pepper, ginger curry, chestnut honey and mimosa flower. A second location on Campo San Tomá offers more cupcakes, mousses, pralines and upscale gift-wrapped treats. (☏041 275 01 49; www.viziovirtu.com; Calle del Campaniel 2898a, San Polo; ☺10am-7.30pm; ☻San Tomà)

Drogheria Mascari
FOOD, WINE

33 🔒 Map p76, G3

Ziggurats of cayenne, leaning towers of star anise and chorus lines of olive oils draw awestruck foodies to Drogheria Mascari's windows. Indoors, chefs clutch truffle jars like holy relics, kids ogle candy in copper-lidded jars and dazed gourmets confront 50 aromatic honeys. For small-production Italian wines – including Veneto cult producers like Quintarelli – don't miss the backroom *cantina* (cellar). (☏041 522 97 62; www.imascari.com; Ruga degli Spezieri 381, San Polo; ☺8am-1pm & 4-7.30pm Mon, Tue & Thu-Sat, 8am-1pm Wed; ☻Rialto)

Alberto Sarria Masks
ARTISANAL, MASKS

34 🔒 Map p76, D2

Go Gaga or channel Casanova at this atelier, dedicated to the art of masquerade for more than 30 years. Sarria's *commedia dell'arte* masks are worn by theatre companies from Argentina to Osaka – ominous burnished black leather for dramatic leads, harlequin-checquered *cartapesta* (papier-mâché) for comic foils, starting from €30. Watch as masks are hand-cast and one-of-a-kind marionettes take their first steps. (☏041 520 72 78; www.masksvenice.com; Calle del Tentor 1807, Santa Croce; ☺10am-7pm; ☻San Stae)

San Polo Vetro
ARTISANAL, GLASS

35 🔒 Map p76, D3

Leaving a fine Veneto vintage unfinished is unforgiveable in Venice, unless you employ a wine-bottle stopper of lampworked glass by Viviana Toso. The artisan can be found at her torch, spinning molten glass into red devils, pink-lipped conch shells, polka-dotted perfume bottles and her signature stoppers in psychedelic shades of orange, sky blue and acid green. (di Viviana Toso; ☏041 71 46 88; Campo San Agostin 2309, San Polo; ☺10.30am-6.30pm Mon-Sat; ☻San Tomà)

La Pedrera
ARTISANAL, JEWELLERY

36 🔒 Map p76, D3

Made you look: these Murano glass jewels in bold colours and essential shapes have the attention-getting powers of traffic lights, and merit a detour between Campo San Polo and Campo San Giacomo dell'Orio. Cascades of lilac beads cluster around the collarbone like wisteria, and a 1920s flapper-inspired drop necklace made with antique scarlet beads demands a Venetian jazz concert. (☏041 244 01 44; www.lapedrera.it; Campo Sant'Agostin 2279a, San Polo; ☺10am-6pm Mon-Sat, 10am-1pm Sun; ☻San Tomà)

Explore

Cannaregio & the Ghetto

Anyone could adore Venice on looks alone, but in Cannaregio you'll fall for its personality. Just off bustling Strada Nuova is the tiny Ghetto, a living monument to the outsized contributions of Venice's resilient Jewish community. Between Gothic beauty Madonna dell'Orto and Renaissance jewel Chiesa di Santa Maria dei Miracoli, footsteps echo along moody Fondamenta Misericordia.

The Sights in a Day

🔆 Detour away from Ponte di Rialto (Rialto bridge) to discover the little neighbourhood corner chapel that marks a turning point in art history: **Chiesa di Santa Maria dei Miracoli** (p98). Wander up Fondamenta Nuove, and turn the corner to glimpse bombastic, baroque church I Gesuiti. Follow aptly named Fondamenta Zen and misnomer Fondamenta della Misericordia towards **Chiesa della Madonna dell'Orto** (p98), bedecked with Tintoretto masterpieces.

☀️ Channel your inner Marco Polo and find far-flung **Anice Stellato** (p98) for stellar trade route–inspired seafood dishes. Explore the tiny island that offered refuge from the Inquisition, bailed out the Venetian empire and sparked a Renaissance in thought: **the Ghetto** (p92), historical home of Venice's Jewish community. Refuel with pistachio gelato at **Gelateria Ca' d'Oro** (p101) before discovering Grand Canal photo ops and stolen masterpieces inside Venetian Gothic palace **Ca' d'Oro** (p98).

🌙 Reserve ahead for dinner at **Ai Promessi Sposi** (p100) or make a meal of *cicheti* (Venetian tapas) instead (p94).

For a local's night in Cannaregio, see p94.

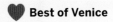

👁 Top Sights

Campo del Ghetto Nuovo & the Ghetto (p92)

🔍 Local Life

Cicheti Circuit (p94)

🖤 Best of Venice

Architecture

Ca' d'Oro (p98)

Chiesa di Santa Maria dei Miracoli (p98)

Schola Spagnola (p93)

Eating

Anice Stellato (p98)

Osteria Alla Vedova (p95)

Getting There

⛴ **Vaporetto** Besides the Ferrovia stop, there are two more Grand Canal stops in Cannaregio: San Marcuola (lines 1, 82 and N) and Ca' d'Oro (1 and N). Lines 41, 42, 51 and 52 head from Ferrovia through Canale di Cannaregio to Fondamenta Nuove. Ferries head from Fondamenta Nuove to the northern islands, including Murano and Burano.

Top Sights
Campo del Ghetto Nuovo & the Ghetto

This Cannaregio corner once housed Venice's *getto* (foundry), but its role as Venice's Jewish quarter from the 16th to 18th centuries gave the word a whole new meaning. Upper storeys were added around Campo del Ghetto Nuovo to house new arrivals, synagogues and publishing houses. The Jewish community stocked and funded Venice's commercial enterprises by day, while at night and on Christian holidays they were restricted to the gated island of Ghetto Nuovo.

◉ Map p96, C3

Synagogue interior

Don't Miss

Schola Italiana

The starkly beautiful wooden cupola of the 1575 Schola Italiana (Italian Synagogue) sits atop private apartments in Campo del Ghetto Nuovo.

Schola Tedesca

According to 16th-century Venetian law, only the German Jewish community could lend money. The Schola Tedesca (German Synagogue) reflects the success of this trade in its baroque pulpit, carved benches and gilded women's gallery, modelled after a Venetian opera balcony.

Schola Canton

The cupola of c1531 Schola Canton (the Corner or French Synagogue) has gilded 18th-century interiors featuring eight charming landscapes inspired by Biblical parables.

Campo del Ghetto Vecchio

Over the bridge in Campo del Ghetto Vecchio are two synagogues with 17th-century interiors attributed to Baldassare Longhena. **Schola Levantina** (Levantine Synagogue) has a magnificent wooden pulpit, while **Schola Spagnola** (Spanish Synagogue) features a sweeping staircase, Venetian high-arched windows and baroque interiors.

Museo Ebraico

At the Ghetto's heart, **Museo Ebraico** (Jewish Museum; Map p96, C3; ☎041 71 53 59; www.museoebraico .it; Campo del Ghetto Nuovo 2902b; adult/reduced €3/2; ⏰10am-7pm Sun-Fri except Jewish holidays Jun-Sep, to 6pm Oct-May; Guglie) explores the history of Venice's Jewish community through everyday artifacts, including finely wrought devotional objects and books published in the Ghetto during the Renaissance.

☑ Top Tips

▶ Museo Ebraico offers guided tours of Schola Tedescha, Schola Canton and either Schola Italiana or still-active Schola Spagnola. Hour-long English-language tours leave from the museum's lobby seven to eight times daily, starting at 10.30am. Museum entry is included with tour tickets.

▶ Schola Levantina is still used for Saturday prayers in winter (it has heating), while Schola Spagnola is used in summer.

▶ Enquire at the Museo Ebraico about guided tours to the Antico Cimitero Israelitico (Old Jewish Cemetery) on the Lido.

✕ Take a Break

Cross the bridge from the Ghetto for inspired *cicheti* at Al Timon (p95) or head to hidden Anice Stellato (p98) for sustainable seafood in a casual canalfront setting.

Local Life
Cicheti Circuit

After lavish canalside Cannaregio lunches, skip three-course dinners and make meals of *cicheti* (Venetian tapas) instead. Platters appear on counters across Cannaregio at 6pm, from perfect €1 *polpette* (meatballs) to top-notch *crudi* (Venetian-style sushi, laced with olive oil and/or aged balsamic vinegar). For bargain gourmet adventures, graze these Cannaregio *cicheti* hotspots.

❶ Tramezzini & DJs at Al Parlamento

Entire university careers and international romances are owed to the powerful espresso, 6pm-to-9pm happy 'hour' cocktails and excellent overstuffed *tramezzini* at **Al Parlamento** (☎041 244 02 14; Fondamenta Savorgnan 511; ⊘8am-midnight Mon-Fri, 6pm-midnight Sat & Sun; 🚤Crea). When they warn you the ham, chicory and pepperspread *tramezzino* (triangular, stacked

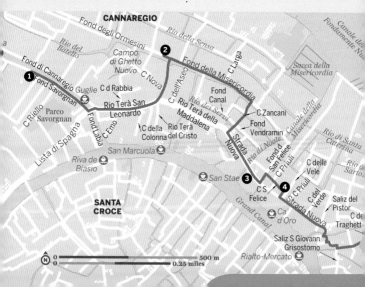

sandwiches made with squishy white bread) is *picante* (spicy), you'd best pre-order that mojito. Thursday brings live music at 9pm, and weekends you'll be talking over DJ sets unless you claim canalside seating early.

❷ Crostini & Concerts at Al Timon

Find a spot on the boat moored along the canal at **Al Timon** (📞041 524 60 66; Fondamenta degli Ormesini 2754; ⏱11am-1am Thu-Tue & 6pm-1am Wed; 🚤Guglie) and watch the parade of drinkers and dreamers arrive for seafood *crostini* (open-face sandwiches) and quality organic and DOC wines by the *ombra* (half-glass) or carafe. Folk singers play sets canalside when the weather obliges; when it's cold, regulars scoot over to make room for newcomers at indoor tables.

❸ Bruschette & Crudi at La Cantina

Talk about slow food: grab a stool and local Morgana beer at **La Cantina** (📞041 522 82 58; Campo San Felice 3689; cicheti €2.50-5, meals €25-40; ⏱11am-11pm Mon-Sat; 🚤Ca' d'Oro) while you await seasonal bruschette made to order and hearty bean soup. Seafood platters require larger appetites and deeper pockets – market price varies, so ask today's rate – but mullet

with roast potatoes, *scampi crudi* (Venetian-style sweet-prawn sushi) and corn-breaded fried anchovies are worthy investments.

❹ Meatballs & Ombre at Osteria Alla Vedova

Culinary convictions run deep here at one of Venice's oldest **osterie** (📞041 528 53 24; Calle del Pistor 3912; cicheti €1-3.50, meals €15-40; ⏱11.30am-2:30pm & 6.30-10.30pm Mon-Wed, Fri & Sat, 6.30-10.30pm Sun; 🚤Ca' d'Oro), so you won't find *spritz* or coffee on the menu or pay more than €1 to snack on a Venetian meatball. Enjoy superior seasonal *cicheti* and *ombre* (wine by the glass) with the local crowd at the bar, or call ahead for brusque table service and strictly authentic Venetian tripe or clam pasta.

❺ Sarde in Saor at Un Mondo di Vino

Get here early for first crack at marinated artichokes and *sarde in saor* (sardines in tangy onion marinade) and claim a few square inches of ledge for your plate and wineglass. **Un Mondo Di Vino** (📞041 521 10 93; Salizada San Canciano 5984a; ⏱11am-3pm & 5.30-11pm Tue-Sun; 🚤Rialto-Mercato) offers 45 wines by the glass, with prices ranging from €1.50 to €5, so take a chance on a freak blend or obscure varietal.

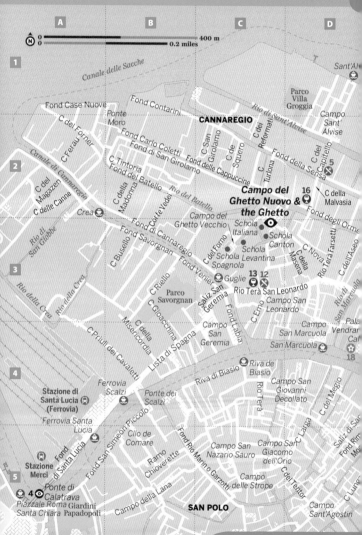

CANNAREGIO

Campo del Ghetto Nuovo & the Ghetto

SAN POLO

For reviews see

Top Sights	p92
Sights	p98
Eating	p98
Drinking	p102
Entertainment	p103
Shopping	p104

Madonna dell'Orto

Madonna dell'Orto

Campiello Piave

Chiesa della
Madonna dell'Orto
Campo della
Madonna dell'Orto

Rio della nna dell'Orto

Fond Gasparo
Contarini

C dei Mori

C Tintoretto

Rio dei Muti

Corte Vecchia

Sacca della
Misericordia

Fond dell'Abbazia

Canale delle Fondamenta Nuove

Canale della Misericordia

C Lunga Santa Caterina

Fond Nuove

Fondamenta Nuove

C de le
Tre Crose

C Larga dei Botteri

Fond Nuove

C del Fumo

Rio della Sensa

C Larga

lla Misericordia

Canal

C Zancani

Rio della Maddalena

Strada Nuova

Bio di Noale

Fond d
San Felice

C della
Racchetta

Rio della Racchetta

C Fond Santa
Caterina Fond Zen

C Marco Foscarini

C dei Specchieri

Rio dei Gesuiti

Campo dei
Gesuiti

C Venier

*Rio di
Santa Sofia*

Rio Terà di
Barba Fruttarol

C dei Volti

C Widmani

Rio Terà dei Birri

Rio della Panada

C del Fumo

C de' Testa

C del Squero

Fond dei Mendicanti

Stae

Grand Canal

po
Stae

Ca' d'Oro

C S Felice

C di Ca'
d'Oro

Ca'
d'Oro

C delle Vele

C Priuli

Strada Nuova

C del Verde

Campo
Santa Sofia

Campo dei
SS Apostoli

Rio dei Santi Apostoli

Campiello
della Cason

Campo
Santa Maria
Nova

Chiesa di Santa
Maria dei Miracoli

C Larga
G Gallina

Campo dei
Miracoli

Campo SS
Giovanni
e Paolo

CASTELLO

*Rio Terà
d'Franceschi*

Campo
San Cassian

Regina

Campo delle
Beccarie

Rialto-
Mercato

Campo San
Giacometto

C Castelli

RIALTO

Sights

Chiesa della Madonna dell'Orto
CHURCH

1 Map p96, E2

This 1365 brick Gothic cathedral was the parish church of Renaissance master Tintoretto, who is buried here. Two of his finest works are in the apse: *Presentation of the Virgin in the Temple,* with starstruck angels and mortals vying for glimpses of Mary, and his 1546 *Last Judgment,* where an angel rescues one last soul from the ultimate *acqua alta*. (Campo della Madonna dell'Orto 3520; admission €3, or Chorus Pass; ⏱10am-5pm Mon-Sat; 🚽; 🚤Madonna dell'Orto)

Chiesa di Santa Maria dei Miracoli
CHURCH

2 Map p96, G5

When Nicolò di Pietro's Madonna icon started miraculously weeping in its outdoor shrine around 1480, crowd control became impossible. With pooled resources and marble scavenged from San Marco slag-heaps, neighbours built this chapel (1481–89) to house the painting. Pietro and Tullio Lombardo's design dropped grandiose Gothic in favour of human-scale harmonies, introducing Renaissance architecture to Venice. (Campo dei Miracoli 6074; admission €3, or with Chorus Pass; ⏱10am-5pm Mon-Sat; 🚤Fondamenta Nuove)

Ca' d'Oro
MUSEUM

3 Map p96, F4

Along the Grand Canal, you can't miss 15th-century Ca' d'Oro's lacy arcaded Gothic facade, resplendent even without the original gold-leaf details that gave the palace its name (Golden House). Baron Franchetti donated to Venice this treasure-box palace packed with masterpieces displayed upstairs in **Galleria Franchetti**, alongside Renaissance wonders plundered from Veneto churches during Napoleon's Italy conquest. (☎041 520 03 45; www .cadoro.org; Calle di Ca' d'Oro 3932; adult/ reduced €6/3; ⏱8.15am-7.15pm Mon-Sat, 9am-12.30pm Sun; 🚤Ca' d'Oro)

Ponte di Calatrava
BRIDGE

4 Map p96, A5

Avant-garde Spanish architect Santiago Calatrava's 2008 bridge over the Grand Canal has been called many things: a fish tail, a glass tongue, unnecessary, overdue, pleasingly streamlined and displeasingly wheelchair-inaccessible. By night the bridge is a ghostly streak of light reflected in the Grand Canal; daylight reveals its red ribbed-steel underbelly. (Ponte della Costituzione; 🚤Piazzale Roma)

Eating

Anice Stellato
VENETIAN $$$

5 Map p96, D2

If finding this obscure corner of Cannaregio seems like an adventure, wait

Understand
Venetian Jewish History

Renaissance in the Ghetto

During the 14th- to 16th-century Italian Renaissance, pragmatic Venice granted Jewish communities the right to practise certain professions key to the city's livelihood, including medicine, trade, banking, fashion and publishing. Despite a 10-year censorship order issued by the Church in Rome in 1553, Jewish Venetian publishers contributed hundreds of titles popularising new Renaissance ideas on humanist philosophy, medicine and religion – including the first printed Qur'an.

Interfaith Enlightenment

Leading thinkers of all faiths flocked to Ghetto literary salons. In the 17th century, the Schola Italiana's learned rabbi Leon da Modena was so widely respected that Christians attended his services. When Venetian Jewish philosopher Sara Copia Sullam (1592–1641) was anonymously accused of denying the immortality of the soul – a heresy punishable by death under the Inquisition – Sullam responded with a treatise on immortality written in two days. The manifesto became a bestseller, and Sullam's writings are key works of early modern Italian literature.

Signs of Restriction

On the wall at No 1131 Calle del Ghetto Vecchio, an official 1704 decree of the Republic forbids Jews converted to Christianity entry into the Ghetto, punishable by 'the rope [hanging], prison, galleys, flogging...and other greater punishments, depending on the judgment of their excellencies (the Executors Against Blasphemy)'. Such restrictions on Venice's Jewish community were abolished under Napoleon in 1797, when some 1626 Ghetto residents gained standing as Venetian citizens.

The Enduring Legacy

Mussolini's 1938 Racial Laws revived discriminatory rules, and in 1943 most Jewish Venetians were deported to concentration camps. As a memorial on the northeast end of the Campo del Ghetto Nuovo notes, only 37 returned. Today few of Venice's 400-person Jewish community actually live in the Ghetto, but its legacy remains in bookshops, art galleries and religious institutions.

Osteria L'Orto dei Mori

until dinner arrives: think pistachio-encrusted lamb chops, succulent house-made prawn ravioli and lightly fried *moeche* (soft-shell crab) gobbled whole. Tin lamps and recycled paper placemats on communal tables keep the focus on local food and local company – all memorable. Book ahead. (☏041 72 07 44; Fondamenta della Sensa 3272; mains €18-23; ☺noon-2pm & 7.30-11pm Wed-Sun; 🛳Madonna dell'Orto)

Ai Promessi Sposi VENETIAN $$

 Map p96, F5

Bantering Venetians thronging the bar are the only permanent fixtures at this newly revived neighbourhood *osteria*, where handwritten menus created

daily feature fresh Venetian seafood and Veneto meats at excellent prices. Seasonal standouts include *seppie in umido* (cuttlefish in rich tomato sauce) and housemade tagliatelle with *anatra* (wild duck), but pace yourself for feather-light tiramisu and elegant chocolate torte. (☏041 241 27 47; Calle d'Oca 4367; meals €25-35; ☺11.30am-3pm & 6-11pm Thu-Sun & Tue, 6-11pm Mon & Wed; 🛳Ca' d'Oro)

Osteria Boccadoro VENETIAN $$$

 Map p96, H5

Birds sweetly singing nearby are probably angling for your leftovers, but they don't stand a chance. Chef-owner Luciano's creative *crudi* (Venetian-

style sushi) are two-bite delights –
tuna with blood orange, sweet prawn
atop tart green apple – and cloudlike
gnocchi topped with spider crab are
gone entirely too soon. Save room for
luxuriant mousse with six kinds of
chocolate. (☑041 521 10 21; www.boccadoro
venezia.it; Campiello Widmann 5405a; meals
€40-55; ☺noon-3pm & 7-10pm Tue-Sun;
☯Fondamenta Nuove)

Gelateria Ca' d'Oro GELATO $

8 Map p96, F5

Foot traffic stops here for Slow Food
flavours artisanally made in-house
daily. Regional Italian flavours are top
choices – especially Sorrento lemon
and extra-creamy Bronte pistachio –
but *sorbetto* (sorbet) in seasonal fruit
flavours like kiwifruit and canteloupe
could turn anyone temporarily vegan.
For a summer pick-me-up, try the
granita di caffe con panna (coffee
shaved ice with whipped cream).
(☑041 522 89 82; Strada Nuova 4273; gelati
€2-4.50; ☺noon-8pm; ♿; ☯Ca' d'Oro)

Osteria
L'Orto dei Mori MODERN ITALIAN $$

9 Map p96, E3

Not since Tintoretto lived next door
has this neighbourhood seen so much
action, thanks to this bustling *osteria*.
Sicilian chef Lorenzo makes fresh
surf-and-turf pasta daily, including
squid atop spinach *tagliolini* and
pasta with zucchini blossoms and
scampi. Upbeat staff and fish-shaped
lamps

set a playful mood, and you'll be
handed *prosecco* (Venetian sparkling
wine) to endure waits for tables; book
ahead. (☑041 524 36 77; www.osteriaorto
deimori.com; Campo dei Mori 3386; meals
€25-45; ☺12.30-3.30pm & 7.30pm-midnight
Wed-Mon; ☯Madonna dell'Orto)

Antica Adelaide TRATTORIA $$

10 Map p96, F4

An old *osteria* with inspired new
ideas, Antica Adelaide combines
hearty lagoon fare served here since
the 18th century with one of Italy's
most exciting menus of small-
production natural wines (eg
biodynamic, organic and using
natural fermentation). Pair lagoon-
clam linguine with organic Cantina
Filippi DOC soave, and *orechiette*
(ear-shaped) pasta with almonds and

Local Life
Menu? What Menu?

At **Dalla Marisa** (Map p96, A2; ☑041
72 02 11; Fondamenta di San Giobbe
652b; set menus €15-35; ☺noon-3pm
& 7-11pm Tue & Thu-Sat, noon-3pm
Mon & Wed; ☯Crea), you'll get no
menu – you'll have whatever
Marisa's cooking – and like it.
Lunches are a bargain at €15 for
a first, main, side, wine, water and
coffee. When you book for dinner,
you'll be informed whether the set
menu is fish-based (usually Tues-
days) or meaty. Reservations and
pre-meal fasting advised.

gorgonzola with Castello di Arcano's sulphite-free organic Refosco blend. (📞041 523 26 29; Calle Priuli 3728; meals €25-40; ⏱7.30-10.30pm; 🚤Ca' d'Oro)

Osteria Da Alberto VENETIAN $

11 🍴 Map p96, H5

All the makings of a true Venetian *osteria* – hidden location, casks of wine, chandeliers that look like medieval torture devices – plus fair prices on spaghetti *alla busara* (with shrimp sauce), seasonal *cicheti,* crispy Venetian seafood fry and silky panna cotta with strawberries. Call ahead, because the kitchen closes early when the joint's not jumping. (📞041 523 81 53; Calle Larga Giacinto Gallina 5401; meals €15-25; ⏱noon-3pm & 6-11pm Mon-Sat; 🚤Fondamente Nuove)

Rizzo SANDWICHES, PASTRIES $

12 🍴 Map p96, C3

Since 1890 Rizzo has been preparing Venetians for train journeys to terra firma with grilled *panini* (sandwiches) packed with garlic-spiked *sopressa* (soft salami) and top-notch San Daniele prosciutto, plus just-baked Burano *esse* (S-shaped biscotti). *Foccace* and *tramezzini* (sandwiches) are rigorously fresh, and the efficient, cheerful *signore* behind the counter sincerely wish you to *torno subito* (return soon), though no convincing is necessary. (📞041 71 83 22; www.rizzovenezia.it; Campo San Leonardo 1355; sandwiches €2.20-5; 🚤Guglie)

Drinking

Torrefazione Marchi CAFE

13 Map p96, C3

Venetians can't catch a train without a pit stop at this aromatic shopfront lined with brass-knobbed coffee bins. Since 1930, Venice's Marchi family has been importing speciality beans, roasted fresh daily in a washtub-size roaster behind the marble bar and ground to order. Even connoisseurs who disdain flavoured brews must try *noxea*, espresso made with coffee beans roasted with hazelnuts. (📞041 71 63 71; www.torrefazionemarchi.it; Rio Terà San Leonardo 1337; ⏱7am-7pm; 🚤Guglie)

Il Santo Bevitore PUB

14 Map p96, E3

San Marco has its glittering cathedral, but beer lovers prefer pilgrimages to this shrine of the 'Holy Drinker' for 14 brews on tap, including Trappist ales and seasonal stouts. The faithful receive canalside seating, footy matches on TV, free afternoon internet access, a saintly *spritz* (prosecco and bitters cocktail) and the occasional live concert (Irish groups and all-girl rock bands are perennial favourites). (📞335 841 57 71; www.ilsantobevitorepub.com; Calle Zancani 2393a; ⏱8am-midnight Mon-Sat; 🚤Ca' d'Oro)

Local Life
Veneto Wine-Tasting

Expand your happy-hour options with an immersion in Veneto wines led by an English-speaking sommelier from **Venetian Vine** (www .venetianvine.com; tastings per person €70 for up to six people). Sessions are usually held at La Cantina (p95) and cover two flights with *cicheti* (Venetian tapas) pairings over two hours – though participants have been known to keep toasting after class.

Algiubagiò   CAFE, BAR

15 | Map p96, H4

Convenient to Murano shoppers and Burano photographers, Algiubagiò offers seaside romance. The long indoor bar is a promising start to date nights, with some 300 wine options and moody spotlighting under the exposed-beam ceiling. Casual drinks may lead to cosy, candlelit tables for two and ambitious (if pricey) meals of goose and truffle ravioli. (☎041 523 60 84; www.algiubagio.net; Fondamente Nuove 5039; ⏰9am-midnight Wed-Mon; ⛴Fonda-mente Nuove)

Agli Ormesini   PUB

16 | Map p96, D2

While the rest of Venice is awash in wine, Ormesini offers more than 100 brews, including reasonably priced bottles of speciality craft ales and local Birra Venezia. The cheery, beery scene often spills into the street – but keep it down, or the neighbours will get testy. (Da Aldo; ☎041 71 58 34; Fondamenta degli Ormesini 2710; ⏰8pm-1am Mon-Sat; ⛴Madonna dell'Orto)

Entertainment

Teatro
Fondamenta Nuove   THEATRE, DANCE

17 ⭐ Map p96, G3

Expect the unexpected in Cannaregio's experimental corner: dances inspired by water and arithmetic, new American cellists and long-lost Kyrgyz composers, Egyptian performance-art premieres in collaboration with Palazzo Grassi, and a steady stream of acclaimed artists from Brazil to Finland playing to a full house of 200. (☎041 522 44 98; www.teatrofondamentanuove.it; Fondamenta Nuove 5013; tickets €2.50-15; ⛴Fondamente Nuove)

Casinò Di Venezia   CASINO

18 ⭐ Map p96, D4

Fortunes have been won and lost since the 16th century inside this palatial casino. Slots open at 11am; to take on gaming tables, arrive after 3.30pm wearing your jacket and poker face. Ask your hotel concierge for free-admission coupons, and take the casino's free water-taxi ride from Piazzale Roma. You must be at least 18 to enter the casino. (Palazzo Vendramin-Calergi; ☎041 529 71 11; www.casinovenezia

.it; Palazzo Vendramin-Calergi 2040; admission €5; ⏲11am-2.30am Sun-Thu, to 3am Fri & Sat; 🚤San Marcuola)

Paradiso Perduto
LIVE MUSIC

19 ⭐ Map p96, E3

'Paradise Lost' is a find for anyone craving a cold beer canalside on a hot summer's night, with occasional live-music acts. Over the past 25 years, troubadour Vinicio Capossela, Italian jazz great Massimo Urbani and Keith Richards have played the small stage at the Paradiso. On Sunday, jam sessions hosted by two independent local labels alternate with local art openings. (☎041 72 05 81; Fondamenta della Misericordia 2540; ⏲6pm-1am Mon & Thu, 11am-1am Fri-Sun; 🚤Madonna dell'Orto)

Shopping

Gianni Basso
ARTISANAL, PRINTER

20 🔒 Map p96, H4

Gianni Basso doesn't advertise his letterpressing services: the clever calling cards crowding his studio window do the trick. Restaurant critic Gale Greene's title is framed by a knife and fork, and Hugh Grant's moniker appears next to a surprisingly tame lion. Bring cash to commission business cards, ex-libris, menus or invitations, and trust Signor Basso to deliver via post. (☎041 523 46 81; Calle del Fumo 5306; ⏲9am-1pm & 2-6pm Mon-Fri, 9am-noon Sat; 🚤Fondamente Nuove)

Understand

Acqua Alta

Acqua alta (high water) isn't an emergency – it's a tide reaching 110cm above normal levels and normally happens four to six times a year, between November and April. *Acqua alta* may cause flooding in low-lying areas, but waters usually recede within five hours.

To see if *acqua alta* is likely, check Venice's Centro Maree 48-hour tidal forecast at www.comune.venezia.it. Alarms sound when *acqua alta* is expected to reach the city within two to four hours:

▶ **One even tone** (up to 110cm above normal): Barely warrants pauses in happy-hour conversation.

▶ **Two rising tones** (110 to 120cm): You might need *stivali di gomma* (rubber boots).

▶ **Three rising tones** (around 130cm): Check Centro Maree online to see where *passarelle* (gangplank walkways) are in use.

▶ **Four rising tones** (140cm and up): Businesses may close early.

De Rossi
ARTISANAL, IRONWORK

21 Map p96, F5

Set a romantic Venetian mood in your own backyard with De Rossi's authentic fisherman's lanterns, a bubble of Murano glass inside a forged-iron frame. This family workshop is among the last, best Venetian lantern-makers, producing traditional and new styles with coloured and matte glass in shapes that range from classic *zucca* (pumpkin) lanterns to sleek modern wall sconces. (☑041 520 00 77; www.derossiferrobattuto.com; Calle del Fumo 5045; ☺10am-7pm Mon-Fri; ☔Ca' d'Oro)

Paolo Olbi
ARTISANAL, PAPER GOODS

22 Map p96, G5

Thoughts worth committing to paper deserve Paolo Olbi's keepsake books, albums and stationery. Ordinary journals can't compare to Olbi originals handmade with heavyweight paper, bound with either hand-tanned or affordable reclaimed leather bindings. Office supplies are upgraded with an embossed winged lion of San Marco, one paw resting on an open book. (☑041 523 76 55; http://olbi.atspace.com; Campo Santa Maria Nova 6061; ☺11.30am-1pm & 3.30-7.30pm; ☔Fondamenta Nuove)

Carta & Design
DESIGN STORE

23 Map p96, E3

Venice aficionados will recognise the architectural silhouettes emblazoned on Roberta Molin's original designs: that's Ponte di Rialto (Rialto bridge)

Local Life
Wagnerian Drama at the Casino

Richard Wagner survived the 20-year effort of composing his stormy Ring cycle only to die at Venice's casino (p103) in 1883. Wagner's suite has been turned into a **museum** (☑041 276 04 07; ☺tours Tue & Sat noon by reservation at least a day in advance). Check the casino website for occasional concerts.

on purple travel journals, the Ca' d'Oro on yellow bookmarks, and the Palazzo Ducale on coloured-pencil sets. Daisy cocktail rings made of rubber and Murano glass deserve a Cannaregio canalside *spritz*, and Venice tote bags enable Strada Nuova shopping sprees. (di Roberta Molin; ☑041 720 514; Strada Nuova 2083; ☺10am-7.30pm; ☔Ca' d'Oro)

Spilli Lab & Shop
CLOTHING

24 Map p96, G5

Glamour comes easily at this Venetian design showcase, with embroidered dresses, graphite wool wrap-dresses and broad-brimmed fedoras. Alessia Sopelsa has an eye for luxe textures and details – yet everything here is surprisingly affordable, with double-digit fashion that commands attention in five-digit Biennale crowds. (☑340 276 72 96; Ponte dei Miracoli 6091; ☺9.30am-12.30pm & 3.30-7.30pm Tue-Sun, 3.30-7.30pm Mon; ☔Fondamente Nuove)

Explore

Castello

Sailors, saints and artists made Castello home to seafood restaurants, ethereal icons and the Biennale. Venice's shipbuilders made seafaring history at the Arsenale; Byzantine churches are gilt to the hilt, luxury hotels line the waterfront and Vivaldi echoes from the orphanage where he worked – but Castello slips into something more comfortable for the Giardini and *bacari* (bars).

The Sights in a Day

☀ Hit heavenly sights across sprawling Castello: rosy Veronese ceilings and Lorenzetti's seafaring Jesus in **Zanipolo** (p110), Negroponte's floating Madonna in Palladio-designed **Chiesa di San Francesco della Vigna** (p110) and Bellini's vibrant Virgin Enthroned altarpiece in opulent **Chiesa di San Zaccaria** (p111).

☀ Empires were launched from the sprawling shipyards of **Arsenale** (p111); if they're not open to visits between Biennale events, historical seafaring adventures await at **Museo Storico Navale** (p112). Sailors still live in Castello around Via Garibaldi, ensuring a steady supply of outstanding seafood lunches at reasonable prices at local *osterie*. After lavish lunches with *vino*, loll in the greenery at **Giardini Pubblici** (p110) and take tea in Napoleon's greenhouse at **La Serra** (p115).

☾ Cover the waterfront along Riva degli Schiavoni for sweeping sunsets reflected in the lagoon, and toast Venice on the balcony at **Bar Terazza Danieli** (p114). In Castello, nights end with epic romance in unlikely places: try a Vivaldi concert in the historical **La Pieta** (p116) orphanage or Collegium Ducale opera arias in Venice's formidable **prison** (p116).

 Best of Venice

Drinking
Bar Terazza Danieli (p114)

La Serra (p115)

Architecture
Palazzo Querini Stampalia (p110)

Biennale Pavilions (p113)

Getting There

⛴ **Vaporetto** Line 1 makes stops along Riva degli Schiavoni, en route from the Lido up the Grand Canal. Line 2 also heads up the Grand Canal. Lines 41, 42, 51 and 52 circle the outer perimeter of Venice, including stops along Riva degli Schiavoni and Giudecca.

A

Rio di S Lio
C del Dose
C de la Malvasia
23
C del Lio
C delle Erbe
C de Pindemonte
14
Rio di San Marina
C Bressana
Saliz San Lio
C Carminati
Fond dei Preti
C Lunga Santa Maria Formosa
Campo Santa Maria Formosa
S Antonio
25
C de la Guerra
Palazzo Querini Stampalia
21
5
C dei Specchieri
C Fiubera
C d Selvadego
Piazza San Marco
SAN MARCO
Piazzetta San Marco
Rio dei Giardinetti
Giardini Ex Reali
San Marco

B

1 Zanipolo
Saliz Santi Giovanni e Paolo
C dell Ospedale
11 Fond Moro
C dei Orbi
18
9 Palazzo Grimani
C di Ruga Giuffa
Palazzo Grimani
Rio di San Saverio
C Corona
C d Chiesa
C d Figher
CASTELLO
Gondola Service
C degli Albanesi
C delle Rasse
20
17
Saliz San Provolo
Campo San Zaccaria
6
Riva degli Schiavoni
Paglia
San Zaccaria

C

Barbaria delle Tole
C delle Cappuccine
C Zon
Rio della Tetta
Borgoloco San Lorenzo
Campo San Lorenzo
Rio di San Lorenzo
C d del Lion
Madonna **Museo delle Icone**
C dei Furlani
10 Saliz dei Greci
Campiello dei Greci
Rio di Greci
Chiesa di San Zaccaria
Rio della Pietà
Pietà
Mon Vittorio Emanuele

D

Chiesa di San Francesc della Vigna
C San Francesc
C San Francesco della Vigna
Rio di Santa Giustina
C Tedeum
4
C San Francesco
Rio di San Francesco
Camp Terr
Saliz San Francesco Corta Nova
C dell'Olio
C M
2 *Scuola di San Giorgio degli Schiavoni*
Fond dei Furlani
C dell'Arco
22
Salizada Sant'Antonio
Campo Bandiera e Mori
C del Pestrin
24
13
C d Erizzo
C Ve
Cllo d Pescaria
12
Riva degli Schiavoni
Riva Ca' di Dio
Arsenale

Bacino di San Marco

Canale di San Marco

San Giorgio

Campo San Giorgio

Isola di San Giorgio Maggiore

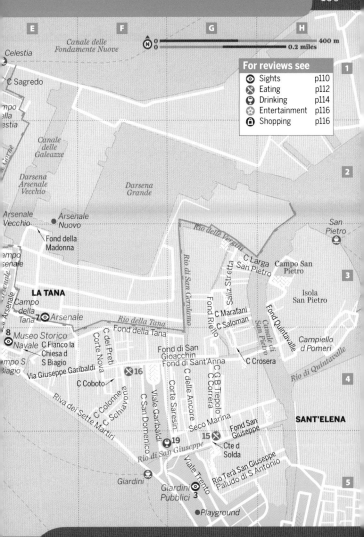

Canale delle Fondamente Nuove

400 m
0.2 miles

Celestia

C Sagredo

Campo ella estia

Canale delle Galeazze

Darsena Arsenale Vecchio

Darsena Grande

San Pietro

Arsenale Vecchio

Arsenale Nuovo

Fond della Madonna

Rio delle Terani

C Larga San Pietro

Campo San Pietro

Isola San Pietro

ampo senale

Rio di San Gerolamo

Saliz Stretta

C Marafani

Fond Quintavalle

Campo della Tana

LA TANA

7 ◉ Arsenale

Fond Riello

C Saloman

Canale di San Pietro

Campiello d Pomeri

8 ◉ Museo Storico Navale

Rio della Tana

Fond della Tana

C Fianco la Chiesa d S Biagio

Corte Nova

C dei Preti

Fond di San Gioacchin

Fond di Sant'Anna

C GB Tiepolo

C Correra

C Crosera

Rio di Quintavalle

ampo S Biagio

Via Giuseppe Garibaldi

C Coboto

✖ 16

C Colonne

C Schiavona

C San Domenico

Viale Garibaldi

Corte Saresin

C delle Ancore

SANT'ELENA

Riva dei Sette Martiri

Seco Marina

Fond San Giuseppe

19 ◉

15 ✖

Rio di San Giuseppe

Viale Trento

Cte d Solda

Giardini

Giardini Pubblici 3 ◉

Rio Terà San Giuseppe

Paludo di S Antonio

● Playground

Sights

Zanipolo

BASILICA

1 ⊙ Map p108, B1

Inside this massive 14th- to 15th-century cathedral are original Murano stained-glass windows and 25 doges' tombs by such notable sculptors as Nicola Pisano and Tullio Lombardo. Paolo Veronese's Cappella del Rosario ceiling depicts the Madonna ascending a staggering staircase, while the second chapel on the right features a Bellini altarpiece. Giambattista Lorenzetti's southwest chapel dome shows Jesus scanning the heavens like a Venetian sea captain. (Chiesa dei SS Giovanni e Paolo; 📞041 523 59 13; www.basilicasantigiovanniepaolo.it; Campo Zanipolo; adult/reduced €2.50/1.25; ⊙9am-6pm Mon-Sat, noon-6pm Sun; 🚤Ospedale)

Scuola di San Giorgio degli Schiavoni

CHURCH

2 ⊙ Map p108, C2

Multicultural Castello was frequented for centuries by Turkish merchants, Armenian clerics, and Balkan and Slavic labourers. This 15th-century religious confraternity headquarters is dedicated to favourite Slavic saints George, Tryphone and Jerome of Dalmatia, whose lives are vividly depicted in minute detail by early Renaissance master colourist Vittore Carpaccio. (📞041 522 88 28; Calle dei Furlani 3259a; adult/reduced €5/3; ⊙2.45-6pm Mon, 9.15am-1pm & 2.45-6pm Tue-Sat, 9.15am-1pm Sun; 👬; 🚤Pietà)

Giardini Pubblici

GARDEN

3 ⊙ Map p108, G5

The city's leafy public gardens are the main home of the Biennale, hosted in pavilions representing global modernist architecture. The playground and other sections are open year-round, and you may be able to wander around to admire the pavilion facades. (www.labiennale.org; 🚤Giardini, Biennale)

Chiesa di San Francesco della Vigna

CHURCH

4 ⊙ Map p108, D1

Designed and built by Jacopo Sansovino with a facade by Palladio, this enchanting Franciscan church is one of Venice's most underappreciated attractions. Bellini's 1507 *Madonna and Saints* illuminates the Cappella Santa, just off the flower-carpeted cloister. Swimming angels and strutting birds steal the scene in the delightful *Virgin Enthroned,* by Antonio da Negroponte (c 1460–70). (📞041 520 61 02; www.sanfrancescodellavigna.it; Campo San Francesco della Vigna 2786; admission free; ⊙9.30am-12.30pm & 3-6pm Mon-Sat, 3-6pm Sun; 🚤Celestia, Ospedale)

Palazzo Querini Stampalia

MUSEUM

5 ⊙ Map p108, B2

Modern meets baroque in this 16th-century palace, donated by Conte Giovanni Querini Stampalia to the city in 1869 and updated by Carlo Scarpa in the 1940s. Today contemporary art

Main entrance, Arsenale

shows and summertime chamber-music concerts give the *palazzo* renewed relevance, and Venice's artiest *aperitivi* are served nightly in the Carlo Scarpa–designed garden and cafe by modernist Mario Botta. (041 271 14 11; www.querinistampalia.it; Campiello Querini Stampalia 5252; 🚤Rialto, San Zaccaria)

Chiesa di San Zaccaria CHURCH

6 Map p108, B3

When 15th-century Venetian girls showed more interest in sailors than saints, they were sent to the convent adjoining San Zaccaria. The wealth showered on the church by their grateful parents is evident. Master-pieces by Bellini, Titian, Tintoretto and Van Dyck crowd the walls. Bellini's altarpiece is such a treasure that Napoleon whisked it away to Paris for 20 years when he plundered the city in 1797. (☎041 522 12 57; Campo San Zaccaria 4693; admission free; ⏰10am-noon & 4-6pm Mon-Sat, 4-6pm Sun; 🚤San Zaccaria)

Arsenale HISTORICAL BUILDING

7 ◉ Map p108, E4

Founded in 1104, the Arsenale housed 300 shipping companies employing up to 16,000 people. These medieval shipyards provided the prototype for industrial assembly lines, turning out a galley a day through strict division of labour. Though often closed to the public, the Arsenale is invaded by arty types for exhibitions and events during Venice's art and architecture Biennales. (☎041 521 88 28; www.labiennale.org; Campo della Tana; adult €20, reduced €12-16; ◷10am-6pm Tue-Sun; ⛴Arsenale)

Museo Storico Navale   MUSEUM

8 ◉ Map p108, E4

Maritime madness spans 42 rooms at this museum of Venice's seafaring history, featuring scale models of Venetian vessels plus Peggy Guggenheim's glamorous gondola. On the ground floor, sprawling galleries display fearsome weaponry and 17th-century dioramas of forts and ports. Upstairs is a sumptuous model of the *bucintoro*, the doge's gilded ceremonial barge, destroyed by Napoleonic troops in 1798. (☎041 244 13 99; Riva San Biagio 2148; adult/reduced €1.55/free; ◷8.45am-1.30pm Mon-Fri, to 1pm Sat; ⛱; ⛴Arsenale)

Palazzo Grimani   MUSEUM

9 ◉ Map p108, B2

After decades of restoration, this Renaissance palace hosts temporary exhibitions inevitably upstaged by its 16th-century frescoes. Predatory birds circle over trompe l'oeil salon forests; snickering grotesques upstage mythological heroes in the dining room; and a stairway cameo depicts original owner Doge Grimani receiving Justice, 40 years after his Inquisition trial for humanist heresy. (☎041 520 03 45; www.palazzogrimani.org; Ramo Grimani 4858; adult/reduced €7/6; ◷8.15am-2pm Mon, 8.15am-7.15pm Tue-Sun; ⛴Ospedale, Rialto)

Museo delle Icone   MUSEUM

10 ◉ Map p108, C2

Glowing colours and all-seeing eyes fill this treasure box of 80+ Greek icons made in 14th- to 17th-century Italy. Keep an eye out for the expressive *San Giovanni Climaco,* in which the saintly author of a Greek spiritual guide is distracted from his work by visions of souls diving into hell. (Museum of Icons; ☎041 522 65 81; www.istitutoellenico.org; Campiello dei Greci 3412; adult/reduced €4/2; ◷10am-5pm; ⛴Pietà)

Eating

Osteria alla Staffa   MODERN VENETIAN $$

11 ✕ Map p108, B1

With fish fresh from the Pescaria, organic produce and artisan cheese, this tiny restaurant offers Venetian classics with a twist. Seafood looks like modernist masterpieces: creamy *baccalà* (cod) graces red radicchio leaves and baby octopi bloom like flowers from a bed of salmon. Reserve ahead, and if you can't find a seat, grab *cicheti* (Venetian tapas) at the bar. (☎041 523 91 60; Calle dell'Ospedale 6397a; meals €20-35; ◷11.30am-3pm & 6-11pm; ⛴Ospedale)

Al Covo   VENETIAN $$$

12 ✕ Map p108, D3

Venetian-Texan couple Cesare Benelli and Diane Rankin have long dedicated their landmark restaurant to the

Understand
Venice Biennale
– –

The world's most prestigious arts show is something of a misnomer: the Venice Biennale (www.labiennale.org) is actually held every year, but the spotlight alternates between art (odd-numbered years, eg 2015, 2017) and architecture (even-numbered years, eg 2014, 2016). The June–October art biennial presents contemporary art at 30 national pavilions in the Giardini Pubblici, with additional exhibitions in venues across town. The architecture biennial is usually held September to November, filling vast Arsenale boat sheds with high-concept structures.

Venice held its first Biennale in 1895 to reassert its role as global taste-maker and provide an essential corrective to the brutality of the Industrial Revolution. At first the Biennale retained strict control, removing a provocative Picasso from the Spanish pavilion in 1910, but after WWII, national pavilions asserted their autonomy and the Biennale became an international avant-garde showcase.

Today international relations never looked better than in Venice's Giardini Pubblici, where Biennale pavilions are purpose-built to reflect national architectural identities from Hungary (futuristic folklore hut) to Canada (ski-lodge cathedral). Inevitably, Venetian modernist Carlo Scarpa steals the show with his cricket-shaped ticket booth.

But the Biennale doesn't stop there. The city-backed organisation also runs the Venice International Film Festival each September and organises an International Festival of Contemporary Dance and concert series every summer. The Biennale hosts experimental theatre and dance performances year-round, sometimes inside historical Arsenale shipyards.

For upcoming event listings, venues and tickets, check the Biennale website. To defray substantial costs to the city, there's an entry fee to the main art and architecture Biennale shows and Venice Film Festival premieres – but many ancillary arts programs are free. When the art biennale's in town, book two months ahead for accommodation, openings and premieres, and at least a week ahead at popular Castello eateries near the Biennale pavilions.

preservation of heritage products and lagoon recipes. Expect pristine lagoon seafood accompanied by artichokes, aubergines, cipollini onions and mushrooms fresh from local island farms, plus well-priced, small-production vintages and succulent Slow Food–accredited meats. (☑041 522 38 12; www.ristorantealcovo.com; Campiello della Pescaria 3968; meals €55-80; ⏱12.45-2pm & 7.30-10pm Fri-Tue; ❄; ⛴Arsenale)

Trattoria Corte Sconta
MODERN VENETIAN $$$

13 Map p108, D3

Well-informed visitors and celebrating locals seek out this vine-covered *corte sconta* (hidden courtyard) for its trademark seafood antipasti and imaginative house-made pasta. Inventive flavour pairings transform the classics: ginger adds zing to lagoon clams; saffron adds a floral note to prawn and courgette linguine. (☑041 522 70 24; Calle del Pestrin 3886; meals €50-65; ⏱12.30-2.30pm & 7-9.30pm Tue-Sat, closed Jan & Aug; ❄; ⛴Arsenale)

Zenzero
CAFE $

14 Map p108, A1

One of the best quick eats in Venice, Zenzero pairs the eye-opening powers of espresso with inventive mini-*panini* (sandwiches) and freshly baked pastries that disappear in a flash. (☑041 241 28 28; http://barzenzero.it; Campo Santa Marina 5902; sandwiches €2-4; ⏱7am-8pm Mon-Fri, to 7.15pm Sat; ⛴Rialto)

Hostaria Da Franz
SEAFOOD $$

15 Map p108, G5

Known in Venice as home to one of the best tiramisus in the world, Da Franz is also a landmark seafood stop (book a month ahead during the Biennale). Don't miss melt-in-the-mouth *seppie* (cuttlefish) prepared in black ink, or *anguila* (eel) prepared according to grandma's secret recipe as a grilled fillet. (☑041 522 08 61; www.hostariadafranz.com; Castello 754, Fondamenta San Giuseppe; ⏱daily; ⛴Giardini)

Le Spighe
VEGETARIAN $

16 Map p108, F4

All vegetarian, all organic and vegan-friendly, this little spot offers quick but delicious eats based on seasonal produce, from crunchy fennel salads to delicious potato-and-squash pies. And the vegan chocolate cake tastes divine, whatever its other virtues might be. (☑041 523 81 73; Via Garibaldi 1341; meals €10-15; ⏱9.30am-2pm & 5.30-7.30pm Mon-Sat; ⛴; ⛴Giardini)

Drinking

Bar Terazza Danieli
HOTEL BAR

17 Map p108, B3

Gondolas glide into dock along the quay, and Palladio's pale San Giorgio Maggiore church suddenly blushes pink: the late-afternoon scene from the Hotel Danieli's top-floor balcony bar definitely calls for a toast. Linger over a *spritz* (*prosecco* and bitters

La Serra

cocktail; €10) or swanky cocktail – preferably the sunset-tinted signature Danieli cocktail of gin, apricot and orange juices, and a splash of grenadine. (☑041 522 64 80; www.starwoodhotels.com; Riva degli Schiavoni 4196; cocktails €18-22; ⊙3-6.30pm Apr-Oct; ⚓San Zaccaria)

Enoteca Mascareta   WINE BAR

18 📍 Map p108, B2

Oenophiles love this traditional *enoteca* for its stellar wines by the glass – including big Amarones and organic *prosecco*. If you're hungry, the excellent *taier misto* (platters of meats and cheeses) could pass for a light meal for two – all for €15. (☑041 523 07 44; Calle Lunga Santa Maria Formosa 5138; meals €30-45; ⊙7pm-2am Fri-Tue; ⚓Ospedale)

La Serra   CAFE

19 📍 Map p108, F5

Order a herbal tisane or the signature pear bellini and sit back amid the hothouse flowers in Napoleon's fabulous greenhouse. Cathedral-like windows look onto the tranquil public gardens, while upstairs workshops in painting and gardening are hosted on the suspended mezzanine. Light snacks and homemade cakes pair with unique microbrews and Lurisia sodas in Slow Food–approved flavours. (Serra dei Giardini; ☑041 296 03 60; www.serradei giardini.org; Viale Giuseppe Garibaldi 1254; snacks €4-15; ⊙11am-8pm Tue-Fri, 10am-9pm Sat & Sun; 🛜♿; ⚓Giardini)

Entertainment

Collegium Ducale   LIVE PERFORMANCE

20 ⭐ Map p108, B3

Spend a perfectly enjoyable evening in prison with this six-member chamber orchestra, whose grace notes in Bach and Albinoni performances escape through the high, barred windows of the converted cell. Opera singers occasionally perform arias with the group, which can get loud in the reverberating stone chamber – bring earplugs for sensitive ears. (☎041 98 42 52; www.collegiumducale.com; Palazzo delle Prigioni; adult/reduced €25/20; ☉shows start 9pm; 🚤San Zaccaria)

Shopping

Sigfrido Cipolato   JEWELLERY

21 🔒 Map p108, A2

Booty worthy of pirates is displayed in this fishbowl-size window display: a constellation of diamonds in star settings on a ring, a tiny enamelled green snake sinking its fangs into a pearl, and diamond drop earrings that end in enamelled gold skulls. Though they look like heirlooms, these small wonders were worked on the premises by master jeweller Sigfrido. (☎041 522 84 37; sigfridocipolato.com; C Casseleria 5336; ☉11am-8pm Tue-Sun; 🚤San Zaccaria)

Understand

Vivaldi's Orphan Orchestras

Over the centuries, Venetian musicians developed a reputation for playing music as though their lives depended on it – which at times wasn't far from the truth. With shrinking 17th-century trade revenues, the state took the quixotic step of underwriting musical education for orphan girls, and the investment yielded unfathomable returns.

Among the maestri hired to conduct orphan-girl orchestras was Antonio Vivaldi (1678–1741), whose 30-year tenure yielded hundreds of concertos and popularised Venetian baroque music across Europe. Visitors spread word of extraordinary performances by orphan girls, and the city became a magnet for novelty-seeking, moneyed socialites.

Modern visitors to Venice can still see music and opera performed in the same venues as in Vivaldi's day – including Tiepolo-frescoed **La Pietà** (Map p108, C3; ☎041 522 21 71; www.pietavenezia.org; Riva degli Schiavoni; adult/reduced €25/20; ☉concerts 8.30pm; 🚤Pietà), the *ospedaletto* (orphanage) where Vivaldi was the musical director.

Banco Lotto 10 FASHION, ACCESSORIES

22 🔒 Map p108, D3

Prison orange is out and plum silk is in at this nonprofit boutique, where fashions are designed and sewn by inmates in a retraining program at the women's prison on Giudecca. La Fenice divas have worn Banco Lotto ensembles, and you can steal the spotlight with smartly tailored jackets (€80 to €140) and opulent handbags made from velvet donated by Fortuny and Bevilacqua. (🖉 041 522 14 39; Salizada da Sant'Antonin 3478a; ⏱ 3.30-7.30pm Mon, 10am-1pm & 4-7pm Tue-Sat; 🚤 Pietà)

Giovanna Zanella SHOES

23 🔒 Map p108, A1

Woven, sculpted and crested like lagoon birds, Zanella's shoes practically demand that red carpets unfurl before you. The Venetian designer custom-makes shoes, so the answer is always: yes, you can get those peep-toe numbers in yellow and grey, size 12, extra narrow. Closed last two weeks of August. (🖉 041 523 55 00; www.giovannazanella.com; Calle Carminati 5641; ⏱ 9.30am-1pm & 3-7pm Mon-Sat; 🚤 Rialto)

Atelier Alessandro Merlin ARTISANAL, CERAMICS

24 🔒 Map p108, D3

Enjoy your breakfast in the nude, on a horse or atop a jellyfish – Alessandro Merlin paints them all on striking black and white cups and saucers. His expressive characters are modern, but the *sgraffito* technique he uses on some of his work dates back to Roman times: scratched white lines against a black background. (🖉 041 522 58 95; Calle del Pestrin 3876; ⏱ 3-7pm Fri & Sun, 10am-noon & 3-7pm Mon-Thu & Sat; 🚤 Arsenale)

Kalimala Cuoieria ARTISANAL, LEATHER

25 🔒 Map p108, A2

Sleek belts with brushed-steel buckles, modern satchels, man-bags and knee-high red boots:Kalimala hand-crafts leather goods in practical, modern styles. Shoes, sandals and gloves are made from vegetable-cured cow hide dyed in earthy tones and vibrant lapis blues. Given the natural tanning and top-quality leather, the prices are remarkably reasonable, with handmade shoes starting at €100. (🖉 041 528 35 96; www.kalimala.it; Salizada San Lio 5387; ⏱ 9.30am-7.30pm Mon-Sat; 🚤 Rialto)

QShop MUSEUM SHOP

(5) 🔒 Map p108, B2

Good looks and smarts too, the Querini Stampalia Foundation shop is a well-curated selection of art books, modernist glass, avant-garde jewellery and designer housewares. Modernist masters, such as Carlo Scarpa, are featured alongside contemporary designs, including Benjamin Hubert's pleated Plicate watches. (🖉 041 523 44 11; Campiello Querini Stampalia 5252; ⏱ 10am-6pm Tue-Sun; 🚤 Rialto, San Zaccaria)

Explore

The Lagoon & the Islands

Other cities have suburban sprawl and malls; Venice has a teal-blue lagoon dotted with photogenic islands and rare wildlife. Outlying islands range from celebrated glass centres and former Byzantine capitols to beach resorts and arty isles, sometimes divided only by a narrow channel.

The Sights in a Day

☀ Plan your trip carefully around your priorities – or it can be tricky to squeeze in Murano glass, Burano photography and Torcello mosaics between peak *vaporetto* (passenger ferry) hours (9am to 5.30pm). Hit Torcello first, and work your way back to Murano – it's easier to reach from Venice if you need to make a return glass-shopping trip.

☀ Enjoy a sunny, leisurely lunch at Torcello's **Locanda Cipriani** (p133) or Mazzorbo's **Venissa** (p132), then hit Murano for an art-glass blitz, snapping up limited-edition modern pieces created with glass-making techniques in use locally since the 8th century. If contemporary art and Palladian architecture are your priorities, save shopping for another day and head to **Chiesa Isola di San Giorgio Maggiore** (p120).

🌙 Enjoy dinner and jazz on Giudecca at **I Figli delle Stelle** (p127). In summer, hop the *vaporetto* to the Lido for DJ sets and concerts on the beach.

For a local's day on the Lido, see p128.

👁 Top Sights

Chiesa di San Giorgio Maggiore (p120)

Basilica di Santa Maria Assunta & Torcello (p122)

🔍 Local Life

Murano Art Glass (p124)

Getting Creative in Giudecca (p126)

Beaches & Bars on the Lido (p128)

Best of Venice

Best-Kept Secrets

Cattedrale di Santa Maria Assunta (p122)

Museo del Vetro (p125)

Museo del Merletto (p132)

Row Venice (p135)

Getting There

🚤 **Vaporetto** Giudecca: lines 2, 41, 42 and N (night) from San Marco or Dorsoduro; San Giorgio Maggiore: line 2 from San Zaccaria; Lido: lines 1, 2, 51, 52, 61 and 62; Murano: line DM from Ferrovia or 13, 41 or 42 from Fondamente Nuove; Burano/Mazzorbo: LN line from Fondamente Nuove or Murano-Faro stop; Torcello: T line from Burano.

Top Sights
Chiesa di San Giorgio Maggiore

Solar eclipses are only marginally more dazzling than Palladio's white Istrian stone church floating on the lagoon. Begun in the 1560s, it reflects ancient Roman temples more than the bombastic baroque of Palladio's day. Inside, ceilings billow with easy grace over a generous nave, its high windows shedding ethereal light on Tintoretto masterpieces. Behind the church, Fondazione Giorgio Cini has restored the cloisters and converted a defunct naval academy into a shipshape contemporary gallery and cultural centre.

Map p130, C3

041 522 78 27

Isola di San Giorgio Maggiore

9am-12.30pm & 2.30-6.30pm Mon-Sat May-Sep, to 5pm Oct-Apr

San Giorgio Maggiore

Choir, Chiesa di San Giorgio Maggiore

Don't Miss

Palladio's Facade

Palladio's radical 16th-century design grafts a triangular Roman temple pediment onto a lofty church facade. Three-quarter columns, incised capitals and sculptural niches add depth and shadow to the white facade. White Istrian stones are set at an angle to catch the afternoon sun.

Tintorettos

Flanking the altar are Tintoretto's uncharacteristically upbeat *Collecting the Manna* and a lively *Last Supper*, where the apostles seem to be keeping a Venetian *osteria* open after hours. Nearby hangs what is considered to be Tintoretto's final masterpiece, the moving *Deposition of Christ*.

Fondazione Giorgio Cini Shows

After escaping the Dachau internment camp with his son Giorgio, Vittorio Cini returned to Venice on a mission to save Isola di San Giorgio Maggiore in 1951. Cini's **foundation** (☑ 041 220 12 15; www.cini.it; Isola di San Giorgio Maggiore; adult/reduced €10/8; ⏲ guided tours in English & French 11am, 1pm, 3pm & 5pm Sat & Sun, in Italian 10am, noon, 2pm & 4pm Sat & Sun; 🚢 San Giorgio Maggiore) restored the island to glory as Venice's most vital centre for contemporary arts.

Monastery Complex

Behind Palladio's church are more treasures restored by Fondazione Cini: a refectory and cloister by Palladio, and Baldassare Longhena's monumental staircase and 17th-century library. The refectory features a video projection of Paolo Veronese's *Nozze di Cana* (Wedding at Cana), which graced this hall until Napoleon's troops brought it in pieces to France; it still hangs in the Louvre.

☑ Top Tips

▶ A lift whisks visitors up the 60m-high bell tower (adult/reduced €3/2) for stirring Venetian panoramas – a splendid alternative to long lines at San Marco's campanile.

▶ Check the Fondazione Cini website for major exhibitions year-round and summertime performances in open-air Teatro Verde.

▶ Weekend tours lead through Borges Labyrinth and Andrea Buora's tranquil 1526 Chiostro dei Cipressi.

✗ Take a Break

For canalfront panoramas and superb seafood, hop the *vaporetto* one stop to Giudecca's I Figli delle Stelle. Family-style lunches are served in the shadow of Palladio's Il Redentore at Giudecca's Al Pontil Dea Giudecca (p133).

Top Sights
Basilica di Santa Maria Assunta & Torcello

On the pastoral island of Torcello, sheep outnumber the 14 or so human residents – you'd never guess this was once a Byzantine metropolis of 20,000, except for the glorious golden mosaics inside Basilica di Santa Maria Assunta. Serenity prevails and wild ducks swoop lazily overhead; it's been a while since Attila the Hun held his stone throne here and Ernest Hemingway brought hunting parties to Torcello's shores.

⊙ Map p130, E1

Piazza Torcello

adult/reduced €5/4, incl museum €8/6

⊙ 10.30am-6pm Mar-Oct, 10am-5pm Nov-Feb

⚲ Torcello

Chiesa di Santa Fosca, Torcello

Don't Miss

Mosaics at Basilica di Santa Maria Assunta

Don't let its serene exterior fool you: the basilica (founded in 639 and reconstructed around 1008) is full of gripping tales told in vivid mosaics. Inside, the Madonna rises above corn poppies like the sun in the golden eastern apse, while the *Last Judgment* looms ominously on the western wall.

Byzantine Civilisation at Museo di Torcello

Relics of Torcello's 7th- to 11th-century Byzantine empire heyday are shown inside 13th-century Palazzo del Consiglio, home to the **Museo di Torcello** (☎041 73 08 75; Piazza Torcello; adult/reduced €3/1.50, incl cathedral €8/5; ☉10.30am-5pm Tue-Sun Apr-Oct, to 5pm Nov-Mar; ⛴Torcello). Exquisite mosaic fragments here show glass mastery achieved in Torcello before Murano entered the business, while upstairs archives contain Greco-Roman artifacts from the lost civilisation of Altinum. Out front you'll spot the worn stone throne Attila the Hun is said to have occupied when he tore through the area in the 5th century.

Shrine to a Teen Rebel at Santa Fosca

Proof that parents just don't understand is found in this 11th-century church. **Chiesa di Santa Fosca** (☉10am-4.30pm; ⛴Torcello) honours a Roman girl raised in Libya who converted to Christianity at 15. Her angry father had her arrested, until an angel frightened the soldiers away. But the teen calmly turned herself in, knowing she'd be tortured to death. In 655, a Venetian sailor named Vitale brought Fosca's remains to Torcello, and they're still enshrined here.

☑ Top Tips

▶ Overnight stays are available at the **Locanda Cipriani** (☎041 73 01 50; www.locandacipriani.com; Piazza Santa Fosca 29, Torcello; per person €100-190, with half board €160-240; ☉closed Tue & Jan; ❉; ⛴Torcello), but reserve well ahead for Hemingway's favourite room with squeaky floorboards and garden views.

▶ Last entry to Santa Maria Assunta is half an hour before closing.

▶ The soaring bell tower offers commanding lagoon views, but was undergoing restoration at the time of writing.

✕ Take a Break

Locanda Cipriani (p133) offers bellinis and duck pasta in a splendid rose garden. Otherwise, hop the T *vaporetto* to Mazzorbo for lagoon-inspired fare on in the vineyard patio Venissa (p132).

Local Life
Murano Art Glass

Unrivalled masters of art glass since the 10th century, Venice's glass artisans moved to Murano in the 13th century to contain *fornace* (furnace) fire hazards. Trade secrets were so jealously guarded that glass masters who left the city were threatened with assassination. Today, Murano glass masters ply their trade along Fondamenta dei Vetrai and Ramo di Mula, and their wares are unmatched.

1 Basilica Bones & Mosaics

In medieval **Basilica dei SS Maria e Donato** (Campo San Donato; admission free; ⊙9am-noon & 3.30-7pm Mon-Sat, 3.30-7pm Sun; 🏛Museo) a 12th-century gilded-glass mosaic Madonna created in Murano's *fornaci* graces the apse and the bones of a dragon hang behind the altar – according to legend the dragon was slayed by San Donato, whose remains also rest here. Underfoot is a 12th-century mosaic floor.

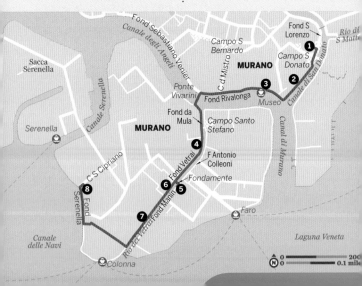

② Glass Museum

Since 1861, **Museo del Vetro** (Glass Museum; ✆041 73 95 86; www.museovetro.visitmuve.it; Fondamenta Giustinian 8; adult/reduced €8/5.50; ⊙10am-6pm Apr-Oct, to 5pm Nov-Mar; ⛴Museo) has presented Murano's glass-making prowess here in Palazzo Giustinian. Downstairs are priceless 1500-year-old examples of iridescent Roman glass; upstairs is the frescoed **Salone Maggiore** (Grand Salon), where displays include a botanically convincing 1930s glass cactus.

③ Davide Penso Beadwork

Davide Penso (✆041 527 56 59; www.davidepenso.com; Fondamenta Rivalonga 48; ⊙10am-5.30pm Mon-Sat; ⛴Museo) has taken the art of bead-making global, with African-inspired necklaces exhibited at Boston's Fine Arts Museum. Lampworked beads in essential shapes are strung onto modern necklaces and bracelets that look ancient.

④ Campagnol & Salvadore DIY

Campagnol & Salvadore (✆041 73 67 72; Fondamenta Vetrai 128a; ⊙10.30am-6pm Mon-Sat; ⛴Colonna) specialises in light-hearted creations: aqua and yellow bead necklaces look like strands of tiny beach balls. Aspiring designers can create their own looks from individual blown-glass beads (€3 to €15 per bead).

⑤ Cutting-edge at ElleElle

Nason Moretti has made modernist magic in glass since the 1950s, and at **ElleElle** (✆041 527 48 66; www.elleelle murano.com; Fondamenta Manin 52; ⊙10am-6pm Mon-Sat; ⛴Colonna) is breaking new ground with collections for New York's MoMA. Prices start at €30 for signed, blown-glass drinking glasses.

⑥ Winged Goblets at Toffolo

Classic gold-leafed winged goblets and mind-boggling miniatures are the legendary master glassblower's trademarks at **Toffolo Gallery** (✆041 73 64 60; www.toffolo.com; Fondamenta Vetrai 37; ⊙10am-6pm Mon-Sat; ⛴Colonna), but you'll also find some dramatic departures: chiselled cobalt-blue vases and highly hypnotic pendants.

⑦ Modern Classics at Venini

Of the big houses, **Venini** (✆041 273 72 04; www.venini.it; Fondamenta Vetrai 47; ⊙9.30am-6pm Mon-Sat; ⛴Colonna) remains the most relevant, defining modernist trends since the 1930s. Recent collaborations feature design greats like Carlo Scarpa and, most recently, Fabio Novembre, who created giant glass 'Happy Pills' for Venini.

⑧ Sent Studio Jewels

The Sent sisters are fourth-generation glassmakers, and their new light-filled, exposed-concrete **Marina e Susanna Sent Studio** (✆041 527 46 65; www.marinaesusannaset.com; Fondamenta Serenella 20; ⊙Sep-Jul; ⛴Colonna) is as strikingly modern as their jewelery: ice-blue glass waterfall necklaces and lava-red beads on paper collars. Ask to open jewelery drawers to browse hidden treasures.

Local Life
Getting Creative in Giudecca

Once the glamorous garden-villa island getaway of Venice's elite, Giudecca became a military-industrial complex in the 19th century. Now its brutalist factories, barracks and arsenals are being creatively repurposed into industrial-cool hubs by Venice's creative class. Whether your creative aspirations are in design, art, cuisine, theatre, architecture, music or photography, Giudecca is an island of inspiration.

① Design Schemes at Fortuny
Find out why Marcel Proust waxed rhapsodic over Fortuny's silken cottons printed with art-nouveau patterns at **Fortuny Tessuti Artistici** (☎041 522 40 78; www.fortuny.com; Fondamenta San Biagio 805; ◷10am-1pm & 2-6pm Mon-Sat; ⛴Palanca). Dream up decor ideas browsing some 260 textile designs, but don't expect to find out how it's done – fabrication methods

have been jealously guarded in the garden studio for a century.

2 Emerging Art at Giudecca 795

Kickstart art collections with original works by emerging local artists at **Giudecca 795** (📞340 879 83 27; www .giudecca795.com; Fondamenta San Biagio 795; ⏱11am-7pm Tue-Sun Apr-Oct, 4.30-7pm Tue-Sun Nov-Mar; ⛴Palanca) – before they get discovered at the Venice Biennale.

3 Organic Cuisine

Find fresh inspiration at this **Thursday organic market** (Fondamenta delle Convertite; ⏱9am-10am Thu; ⛴Palanca), where the organic produce is grown by farmers who happen to be inmates at the adjacent women's correctional facility. Proceeds help pay for job retraining and post-release reintegration, so the plant-based cosmetics sold here really do work wonders.

4 Arsenal Theatrics

Make art, not war at this former arsenal creatively repurposed as a theatre. **Teatro Junghans** (📞041 241 19 74; www .teatrojunghans.it; Piazza Junghans 494; prices vary; 👶; ⛴Redentore) stages original works and offers workshops on costume design, mask-acting and *commedia dell'arte* (archetypal comedy) – check the online calendar for performances.

5 Triumph at Il Rendentore

Palladio's 1577–92 **Il Redentore** (Chiesa del SS Redentore; Campo del SS Redentore 194; admission €3, or Chorus Pass; ⏱10am-5pm Mon-Sat) church is a triumph of white marble celebrating the city's deliverance from the Black Death. Inside above the portal, Paolo Piazza's strikingly modern 1619 *Gratitude of Venice for Liberation from the Plague* shows the city held aloft by angels in sobering shades of grey.

6 Photography at Tre Oci

The view of San Marco from the three porthole windows at **Casa dei Tre Oci** (📞041 220 12 11; www.fondazionedivenezia .org; Fondamente della Croce 43; admission free; ⏱10am-6pm during exhibitions only; ⛴Zitelle) may inspire your own photographic masterpieces, as may the shows of contemporary photography and art held here. Once the home of early-20th-century artist and photographer Mario de Maria, this neo-Gothic landmark is now a cultural center run by Fondazione di Venezia.

7 Jazz at I Figli delle Stelle

Venice's top jazz musicians play weekend nights along the Giudecca Canal at **I Figli delle Stelle** (📞041 523 00 04; www.ifiglidellestelle.it; Zitelle 70; meals €30-40; ⏱12.30-2.30pm & 7-10pm Tue-Sun, closed mid-Nov–mid-Mar; ⛴Zitelle). Also a talented musician, Pugliese chef Luigi's improvisational skills are obvious in inventive *cicheti* (Venetian tapas) such as *crostini* (toast) with fig jam and liver mousse, and in velvety-smooth homemade pasta.

Local Life
Beaches & Bars on the Lido

Beach chairs and bronzed life-guards may seem a world away from muggy Venice in summer, but they're only a 15-minute ferry ride away. Sandy beaches line the seaward side of the Lido; they're packed in summer but surprisingly clean (they earned 2012 Blue Flag eco-accreditation) and their gentle gradient makes them safe for kids. For adults, there's refreshing cocktails and epic summer-weekend DJ sessions and beach concerts.

1 Beach-hop by Bicycle

To tour at your own pace, rent a set of wheels from friendly **Lido on Bike** (041 526 80 19; www.lidoonbike.it; Gran Viale 21b; bikes per 90min/day €5/9; 9am-7pm mid-Mar–Oct; Lido). Reasonable prices include a free map with recommended routes. Identification showing you're at least 18 is required.

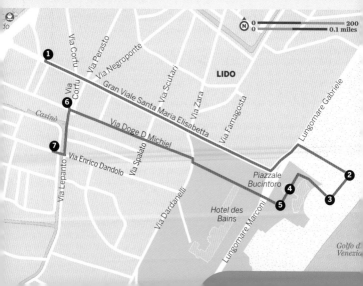

2 Lido Beaches

Beach balls and bronzer make the rounds of **Lido beaches** (Lido di Venezia; deposit/chair/umbrella & chair/hut €5/6/11/17; ⏰most beaches 9.30am-7pm May-Sep; 🚊Lido). The main sandy strip on the sea-facing side is best for castle-building, body-surfing and people-watching – but on sunny weekends, it can get packed. Most beaches charge for chair, umbrella and/or cabana rental, but the crowds thin out and rates drop after 2pm.

3 Be Active at B.each

Warm summer days flow into hot summer nights at **B.each** (Lungomare D'Annunzio 20; ⏰9am-9pm Mon-Tue, Thu & Sun, to 2am Wed & Fri-Sat May–mid-Sep; 🚊Lido) with a parade of diversions: free library books, designated beach sport, massage, live-music sets and open-air cinema. Weekend DJ sets will keep you dancing until you face-plant on a four-poster beach bed.

4 Summer Events at Blue Moon

From afar, the domed semicircular structure of **Blue Moon** (Piazzale Bucintoro 1; admission free; ⏰10am-6.30pm May-Sep; 👬👫; 🚊Lido) looks like an alien landing on the *spiaggia comunale* (public beach) at the north end of the Lido. A series of ramps and staircases lead to a bar, a restaurant, a raised dance floor and a viewing platform. In summer the hive-like structure hums with daytime events and activities.

5 Happy Hour on El Pecador

No you're not suffering from heat stroke: that really is a red, double-decker bus parked along the Lungomare, attracting an alternative crowd to impromptu beach parties. Head to **El Pecador** (Lungomare Gabriele d'Annunzio; sandwiches €2.50-5; ⏰11am-3am May-Sep; 🚊Lido) for some of the Lido's finest stuffed sandwiches and *spritz,* and claim a seat on the canopied top deck.

6 Aperitivi at Jeroboam

With its gleaming wooden bar lined with multicoloured booze bottles, bustling **Jeroboam** (Piazzetta Lepanto 1l; sandwiches & salads €2.50-5; ⏰7.30-2am Wed-Mon; 🚊Lido) is a year-round favourite. Come for coffee in the morning, generous sandwiches and salads at lunchtime and the best Manhattan and aperitivo bar on the Lido in the early evening.

7 Drink Like a Fish at al Mercà

Located in the old Lido fish market, **al Mercà** (📞041 526 45 49; Via Enrico Dandolo 17a; cicheti €2.50-3.50, meals €15-25; ⏰10.30am-3pm & 6-10pm Tue-Sun; 🚊Lido) is a year-round draw for its abundant *cicheti,* outdoor seating and well-priced wine by the glass. Take a pew at one of the marble counters and order up a seafood storm of *folpetti* (mini octopus), fried *schìe* (shrimp) and creamy salt cod.

For reviews see

Canale di Burano

Palude di Torcello Cetrega

Via Fausta

Punta Sabbioni

Porto del Lido

◉ **Basilica di Santa Maria Assunta & Torcello** 9

8

6

Torcello

Burano

Isola di San Francesco del Deserto

Sant'Erasmo

Canale di Treporti

Mazzorbo

Isola della Madonna del Monte

Isola Buel del Lovo

Litorale di Sant'Erasmo

Punta Langa

Isola di San Giacomo in Palude

Le Vignole

Idroscalo Sant'Andrea

Lido di Venezia

◉ **Antico Cimitero Israelitico** 12

Punta Carbonera

V E N E Z I A

Palude del Monte

Isola di Tessera

Isola La Certosa

Canale di San Marco

Isola di San Servolo

5 11 2

3

14 13

7

Murano

Cimitero

Isola di San Michele

1

Sacca Serenella

◉ **Chiesa di San Giorgio Maggiore**

◉ Camo di San Marco

Isola di San Giorgio Maggiore 4

Isola la Grazia

Isola di San Clemente

◉ **Bauer Palladio Spa**

Isola di Campalto

Porto di Campalto

Isola di San Secondo

Grand Canal

Stazione di Santa Lucia (Ferrovia)

Canale della Giudecca

Isola della Giudecca 10

15

Sacca Fisola

L A G U N A

Via Orlanda

Canale Osellino

Porto Marghera

Isola di Tronchetto

Isola di Tresse

Ponte della Libertà

Canale della Giudecca

Isola di San Giorgio in Alga

Isola di Sant'Angelo

Fusina

Sights

Cimitero
HISTORIC SITE

1 Map p130, C3

Napoleon built Venice's island cemetery, and today, goths, incorrigible romantics and music-lovers pay respects here to Ezra Pound, Joseph Brodsky, Sergei Diaghilev and Igor Stravinsky. Architecture buffs visit Codussi's 15th century **Chiesa di San Michele in Isola** and David Chipperfield Architects' austere new **Courtyard of the Four Evangelists** – a sunken bunker with a concrete colonnade and basalt-clad, Gospel-engraved walls. (admission free; ☺7.30am-6pm daily Apr-Sep, to 4pm Oct-Mar; 🚢Cimitero)

Malamocco
TOWN

2 Map p130, D4

A miniature version of Venice right down to the lions of St Mark on medieval facades, Malamocco was actually the lagoon capital from 742 to 811. Pass over Ponte di Borgo to explore its tiny ancient canals, *calli* (lanes), and local-specialty *malamocchina cicheti* at Al Ponte di Borgo (p134). (🚢Lido)

Antico Cimitero Israelitico
CEMETERY

3 Map p130, D4

This quiet, overgrown garden on the Lido was Venice's main Jewish cemetery from 1386 until the 18th century, when a new cemetery was built on Via Cipro. The tombstones were rediscov-

Cimitero

ered in the 1920s; tours aid preservation efforts. Headstone designs range from Venetian Gothic to distinctly Ottoman. (☎041 71 53 59; www.museo ebraico.it; Riviera San Nicolò; group tours adult/ student €10/8, individual tours €80; ☺by reservation Apr-Oct; 🚢Lido, San Nicoló)

Bauer Palladio Spa
SPA

4 Map p130, C4

After a long day of palace museum–hopping, cross the canal to unwind in this serene spa. The Palladio-designed former nunnery offers baths of milk, honey and rose petals (€90) with complimentary jacuzzi and marble steam-room access. (☎041 5207022; www.palladiohotelspa.com; Fondamenta della Croce 33; 🚢Zitelle)

WOODYSTOCK / ALAMY ©

Eating

Le Garzette   FARMSTAY $$

5   Map p130, C4

Nestled amid gardens overflowing with red radicchio, fennel and pumpkins is this rust-red *agriturismo* (farm-stay accommodation). Choose between meat or fish menus and prepare for a parade of organic dishes: crepes plump with asparagus, lightly fried Malamocco artichokes and pear tart made with farm eggs. If you aren't staying the night, reservations are essential for the restaurant. (041 712 16 53; www.legarzette.it; Lungomare Alberoni 32; meals €35-45; 12.30-2.30pm & 7-10.30pm mid-Jan–mid-Dec; ; Lido)

Venissa   MODERN VENETIAN

6   Map p130, E1

An ancient Mazzorbo vineyard deliciously repurposed in 2006 as a destination restaurant and six-room guesthouse earns acclaim for creative, ultra-local lagoon cuisine in an unexpected setting, 50 minutes by boat yet worlds apart from San Marco. The revived vineyard now grows 600-year-old Dorona grapes, yielding a rare golden wine best enjoyed with lagoon langoustine and salicornia seaweed on the patio. (041 527 22 81; www.venissa.it; Fondamenta Santa Caterina 3; noon-3pm & 7-9.30pm Tue-Sun; Mazzorbo)

Acquastanca   OSTERIA $$

7   Map p130, C3

This historic Murano bakery has been reinvented in marble, concrete and brushed steel. Inventive cooking includes plump prawns in a web of filo pastry, exquisite tuna tartare and homemade gnocchi with scallops. At the generous bar, grab a coffee and homemade cake in the morning or wine and cheese in early evening. (041 319 51 25; www.acquastanca.it; Fondamenta Manin 48; meals €30-40; 9am-8pm Tue-Sun, to 10pm Fri; Faro)

Local Life
Colourful Burano

Photographers pack the 50-minute Laguna Nord (LN) ferry ride from Fondamente Nuove for snapshots of pea-green stockings drying between Burano's hot-pink, royal-blue and caution-orange houses.

Burano is locally famed for fishing, lemony S-shaped *buranelli* biscuits and handmade lace, show cased at newly renovated **Museo del Merletto** (Map p130, E1; Lace Museum; 041 4273 0892; www.visitmuve.it; adult/reduced €5/3.50; 10am-6pm Tue-Sun Apr-Oct, to 4.30pm Nov-Mar; Burano), where local lacemakers plying their craft. For handmade Burano lace, visit **Emilia** (Map p130, E1; 041 73 52 99; www.emiliaburano.it; Piazza Galuppi 205; Burano).

During the May/June **Vogalonga** (www.vogalonga.com), sit on the waterfront with a bottle of *prosecco* to cheer rowers making the 32km 'long row' from central Venice to Burano and back.

Trattoria al Gatto Nero

SEAFOOD $$

 Map p130, E1

Once you've tried the homemade *tagliolini* (flat pasta) with spider crab, whole grilled fish, and perfect house-baked Burano biscuits, the ferry ride to Burano seems a minor inconvenience – a swim back here from Venice would be worth it for that decadent langoustine risotto alone. Call ahead and plead for canalside seating. (☏041 73 01 20; www.gattonero.com; Fondamenta della Giudecca 88; meals €30-40; ☺noon-3.30pm & 7.30-10pm Tue-Sun; ⛴Burano)

Locanda Cipriani

ITALIAN $$$

 Map p130, E1

Since 1934 the Cipriani family (of Harry's Bar fame) has run Locanda Cipriani, Hemingway's Torcello retreat for writing, hunting and drinking (not necessarily in that order). Pull up a seat fireside or in the rose garden, feast on the €45 Torcello lunch featuring wild game and enjoy original-recipe bellinis at less than Harry's Bar prices. (☏041 73 01 50; www.locandacipriani.com; Piazza Santa Fosca 29; meals €40-55; ☺by reservation, closed Tue & Jan; ⛴Torcello)

Al Pontil Dea Giudecca

VENETIAN $

 Map p130, C4

Asking for a menu at this Giudecca spot is like asking for one at your

Understand
Liberty on the Lido

Between 1850 and WWI the Lido was the world's most exclusive seaside resort, with decadent Stile Liberty (art-nouveau) villas showing off voluptuous curves and wraparound ironwork balconies along the shoreline. At the south end of Lido's beach is Count Volpi's Ottoman-inspired, Fortuny-decorated 1908 Grand Hotel Excelsior. Mid-strip is 1909 Grand Hotel des Bains, which inspired Thomas Mann's scandalous *Death in Venice* but is currently closed as part of a €330 million Lido redevelopment scheme. Plot your own Liberty walking tour with itineraries available at www2.comune.venezia.it/lidoliberty.

grandma's house. You'll have one of the three daily specials and by the time lunch is over you'll feel as though you should offer to help tidy up. For €12 you can expect a generous plate of pasta, a savoury meat or fish dish, a *contorno* (veggie side dish) and a view of Venice – if you get the one window seat. The bar is open for *cicheti* all day, but meals are only available at lunchtime Monday to Friday. (☏041 528 69 85; Calle Redentore 197a; meals €15; ☺8am-8pm Mon-Sat; ⛴Redentore)

Al Ponte di Borgo

VENETIAN $

11 Map p130, D4

This Malamocco trattoria draws local crowds for abundant *cicheti* including *nervetti* (nerves with onion) and baby squid with the obligatory *prosecco*. Out back beneath the ramshackle pergola, bowls brim with pasta *alla malamocchina* (with mussels, tomatoes, oregano and smoked cheese). (041 77 00 90; Rio Terà Mercerie 27; meals €20-25; 12.30-2.30pm & 7-10pm Tue-Sun Apr-Oct; Lido)

La Favorita

SEAFOOD $$$

12 Map p130, D4

Come here for long Lido lunches, fine wine and impeccable service. Seasonal favorites include *rhombo* (turbot) simmered with capers and olives, spider-crab *gnochetti* (mini-gnocchi) and fish risotto. Book ahead for the wisteria-filled garden and well ahead during the film festival. (041 526 16 26; Via Francesco Duodo 33; meals €35-50; 12.30-2.30pm & 7.30-10.30pm Wed-Sun, 7.30-10.30pm Tue, closed Jan–mid-Feb; Lido)

STEVENS FREMONT / CORBIS ©

Skyline Rooftop Bar

Busa alla Torre SEAFOOD $$

13 Map p130, C2

Murano's classic eatery draws punters with its sunny disposition and €13 set menu. Arrive early for piazza seating with tempting views of glass showrooms, and settle in for seasonal lagoon treats like fried *moeche* (lagoon crab) cooked with pine nuts and sultanas and *tagliatelle* (ribbon pasta) with lagoon *canòce* (mantis prawn). (☑041 73 96 62; Campo Santo Stefano 3; meals €35-50; ☺11.45am-3.30pm; ☻Faro)

Gelateria al Ponte GELATO, SANDWICHES $

14 Map p130, C2

Toasted prosciutto-and-cheese *panini* (sandwiches) and gelato at Murano's Gelateria al Ponte don't cut into glass-buying budgets – sandwiches run at €3 to €5 and ice cream €2. (☑041 73 62 78; Riva Longa 1c; snacks €2-5; ☺9am-5pm Mon-Sat; ♿; ☻Museo)

Drinking

Skyline Rooftop Bar BAR

15 Map p130, B4

From white-sneaker cruise passengers to the €1000-sunglasses set, the rooftop bar at the Hilton Molino Stucky wows everyone with its vast panorama over Venice and the lagoon, with drink prices to. match. From May to September, the bar offers a lunch buffet from noon to 3pm. (☑041 272 33 11; www.molinostuckyhilton.com; Fondamenta San Biagio 810; ☺noon-3.30pm & 6pm-1am; ☻Palanca)

Local Life
Boating on the Lagoon

High-sea adventures are over-rated. Learn to row a *sandolo* (gondola-like rowboat) with Jane Caporal and her team at **Row Venice** (☑345 241 52 66; www.rowvenice .com; 2hr lessons 1-2 people €80, 4 people €120).

Laguna Eco Adventures (☑329 722 62 89; www.lagunaecoadventures .com; 2-8hr trips per person €40-150) offers a day circuit around islands onboard a *bragozzo* (Venetian barge) or a sunset tour of canals in a slim *sanpierota* (twin-sail boat).

Spot rare lagoon wildlife, admire Burano and Torcello architecture and moor for a fish-stew lunch via motorised *bragosso* with **Terra e Acqua** (☑347 420 50 04; www .veneziainbarca.it; ☺day-long trips incl lunch for 9-12 people €380-460; ♿).

Book ahead, bring sunscreen and check weather forecasts – trips are subject to suitable climatic conditions.

The Best of
Venice

Venice's Best Walks

Venice's Best...

Ca' d'Oro (p98)
SYLVAIN SONNET / CORBIS ©

Best Walks
San Marco Royal Tour

🏃 The Walk

Dukes and dignitaries had the run of San Marco for centuries, and now it's your turn on this royal tour that ends with your own palace intrigue.

Start Piazzetta San Marco

Finish I Rusteghi

Length 2.5km; 1¼ hours

✕ Take a Break

Eat and drink like royalty at **I Rusteghi** (Map p34, F1; 📞 041 523 22 05; http://www.osteriairusteghi.com/; Corte del Tentor 5513; mini-panini €2-5; 🕙 10.30am-3pm & 6-11.30pm Mon-Sat; 👶; 🚤 Rialto), with prosciutto platters and Amarone as dark-red and powerful as a doge's cap.

Piazzetta San Marco (p22)

❶ Columns of San Marco

Venetians still hurry past these granite pillars, site of public executions for centuries.

❷ Palazzo Ducale

Pass by the **Ducal Palace** (p28) loggia, where punishments were once publicly announced before they were posted on the palace door.

❸ Piazza San Marco

In **Piazza San Marco** (p22), turn your back on **Basilica di San Marco** (p24) to face Ala Napoleonica, the palace Napoleon brazenly razed San Geminiano church to build. Today it houses the entry to **Museo Correr** (p36); the museum proper occupies the upper storeys of the Scamozzi-designed, Longhena-completed Procuratie Nuove. The right-hand arcade flanking the piazza is Mauro Codussi's 16th-century Procuratie Vecchie.

❹ Chiesa di Santa Maria del Giglio

Take Calle Larga XXII Marzo towards this

ALESSANDRO GUERANI PHOTOGRAPHY / GETTY IMAGES ©

baroque **church** (p37), sculpted with maps charting Venetian vassal states c 1678–81.

5 Chiesa di Santo Stefano

Further west, the bell tower of 15th-century **Santo Stefano** (p38) leans 2m, as though it's had one *spritz* too many. Nearby, Bartolomeo Bon's marble Gothic portals grace brick Chiesa di Santo Stefano.

6 Teatro La Fenice

Follow Calle Caotorta to **Teatro La Fenice** (p43), veering left onto Calle dei Assassini. Corpses were so frequently found here that in 1128 Venice banned the full beards assassins wore as disguises.

7 Palazzo Contarini del Bovolo

Snogging in *campi* (piazzas) is such an established Venetian pastime it's surprising dogi didn't tax it – but duck into Renaissance **Palazzo Contarini del Bovolo** (p38) courtyard for privacy.

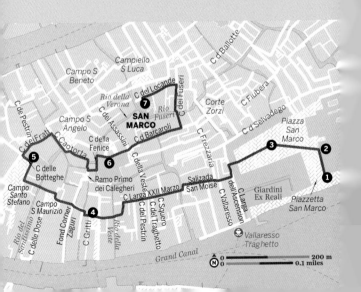

Best Walks
Venice Culinary Adventure

🏃 The Walk

Before there were painters, opera divas or dogi In Venice, there were fishmongers and grocers at the Rialto, bragging shamelessly about their wares. Today, the trade-route cuisine they inspired fills this corner of Venice with delectable discoveries for all your senses. Follow your growling stomach to find them on this culinary walking tour.

Start Rialto Market

Finish Al Prosecco

Length 3.25km; two hours

🍴 Take a Break

Duck into **All'Arco** (Map p76, G3; ☎ 041 520 56 66; Calle dell'Ochialer 436; cicheti €1.50-4; ☺ 8am-3.30pm Mon-Sat, plus 6-9pm Apr-Oct, closed Jul & Aug; 🚤 Rialto-Mercato) for the city's best *cicheti* (Venetian tapas). Ask for *una fantasia* (a fantasy), and father-son chefs Francesco and Matteo will invent a dish with ingredients you just saw at the market.

❶ Rialto Market

A trip through gourmet history starts at this **market** (p72), with its roofed Pescaria, where fishmongers artfully arrange the day's catch atop hillocks of ice.

❷ Drogheria Mascari

Glimpse trade-route treasures that made Venice's fortune at this gourmet **showcase** (p89). Spice pyramids grace shop windows, while speciality sweets are dispensed from copper-topped apothecary jars.

❸ Aliani

Displays of local San Daniele ham and Taleggio cheese at **Aliani** are reminders that Veneto's culinary fame wasn't built on seafood and spices alone.

❹ Cárte

Wander northwest to this tiny **studio-boutique** (p74) to browse lagoon-rippled, marble-paper recipe albums, and dress for dinner with hypnotic paper-cocktail rings.

RICHARD GOERG / GETTY IMAGES ©

Rialto Market (p72)

⑤ Veneziastampa

Cross a couple of bridges until you smell ink drying on letterpress menus and cookbook ex libris labels at **Veneziastampa**.

⑥ Museo di Storia Naturale di Venezia

Learn the scientific names of the lagoon creatures you spotted at the market at Venice's **museum of natural history (p78)**, housed in a Grand Canal palace that was once the Turkish trading-house. It's filled with curious specimens, but architecture made from shellfish and fishbones steals the show.

⑦ Riva di Biasio

Walk this sunny Grand Canal footpath allegedly named for 16th-century butcher Biagio (Biasio) Cargnio, whose sausages contained a special ingredient: children. When found out, Biasio was drawn and quartered.

⑧ Alaska

Now that you've worked up an appetite, try a local speciality (besides sausages). Venetians swear by the mood-enhancing properties of the handmade, organic, roasted-pistachio gelato at **Alaska (p81)**.

⑨ Al Prosecco

Happy-hour temptations ring nearby Campo San Giacomo dell'Orio, but gourmet adventures deserve natural-process *prosecco* (Venetian sparkling wine) toasts at **Al Prosecco (p83)**.

Best Walks
Castello's Byways

🏃 The Walk

Leave the crowds and cramped quarters of San Marco behind, and stretch your legs on a sunny stroll through Castello, where saints and sailors come with the territory.

Start Zanipolo (Chiesa di SS Giovanni e Paolo)

Finish Giardini Pubblici

Length 6.5km; three hours

🍴 Take a Break

After your walk, enjoy a heavenly herbal tisane inside Napoleon's greenhouse at **La Serra** (Serra dei Giardini; Map p108, F5; 📞 041 296 03 60; www .serradeigiardini.org; Viale Giuseppe Garibaldi 1254; snacks €4-15; ⏰ 11am-8pm Tue-Fri, 10am-9pm Sat & Sun; 📶 ♿; 🚊 Giardini) – or a sailor-size *spritz* (*prosecco* and bitters cocktail) and lagoon-front seat to watch boats drift past at **Paradiso** (📞 041 241 39 72; Giardini della Biennale 1260; ⏰ 9am-7pm, later during Biennale; 🚊 Biennale).

JON ARNOLD / GETTY IMAGES ©

Riva degli Schiavoni

❶ Zanipolo

Rising above Castello's tallest ship-masts is Gothic **Zanipolo** (p110) cathedral. In Giambattista Lorenzetti's Jesus the Navigator dome, Jesus plots the course to heaven like a Castello sea captain.

❷ Ospedaletto

A block east, you can't miss statue-bedecked **Ospedaletto**, a 1660s orphanage designed by Palladio and Longhena. This refuge was once famed for its orchestra of orphan girls; today it functions as an aged-care facility.

❸ Chiesa di| San Francesco della Vigna

Continue down Barbaria delle Tole, then dog-leg left to see Palladio-collonaded **Chiesa di San Francesco della Vigna** (p110), where Antonio Negroponte's Madonna and child float like a hovercraft above Venice's lagoon.

❹ Arsenale

Heading south, you'll bump into the massive walls of **Arsenale** (p111), Venice's legendary shipyard. Arsenale's Porta Magna (Main Gate) is considered the city's earliest Renaissance structure. By 1797 Arsenale naval production had dwindled, and La Serenissima surrendered to Napoleon without a fight.

❺ Chiesa di San Martino

Turn right at Campo de le Gorne and follow the walls to this **church** dedicated to San Martino, patron saint of wine and soldiers. By the doorway is the

bocca di leoni (mouth of the lion), a slot where Venetians slipped denunciations of their neighbours. *Arsenalotti* (Arsenale workers) were sworn to silence about trade secrets, since loose lips could sink ships – so reckless talk in Castello bars could be reported as high treason, punishable by death.

❻ Riva degli Schiavoni

From here, turn south onto Castello's breathtaking waterfront promenade, **Riva degli**

Schiavoni, to admire sweeping views across the lagoon.

❼ Giardini Pubblici

The Napoleonic public gardens are dotted with **Biennale** (p113) pavilions, thronged summer through fall with artists, architects and admirers from around the world. Between Biennales, enjoy this unexpected oasis and its avantgarde architecture.

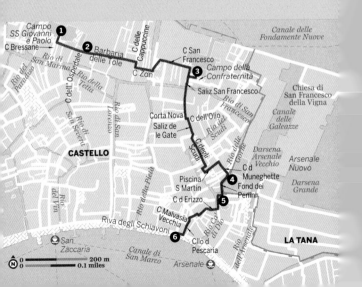

Best
Eating

The visual blitz that is Venice tends to leave visitors bug-eyed, weak-kneed and grasping for the nearest *panino* (sandwich). But there's more to La Serenissima than simple carb-loading. For centuries Venice has gone beyond the call of dietary duty, lavishing guests with inventive feasts. Today visitors enjoy impressive *cicheti* (Venetian tapas), creative trade-route cuisine and a lagoon's worth of seafood.

Cicheti

The city knows how to put on a royal spread, as France's King Henry III once found out when faced with 1200 dishes and 200 bonbons. Today such feasts are available in miniature, from 6pm to 8:30pm, when bars mount lavish spreads of *cicheti*. Prices range from €1 for tasty meatballs to €6 for panchette-wrapped lagoon prawns and white asparagus, typically devoured standing up or atop bar stools.

Authentic Venetian Fare

Save room and time for a proper sit-down Venetian feast, with lagoon seafood, island-grown ingredients and Veneto wine. Here's one foolproof way to distinguish a Venetian eatery from an imposter: lasagne, spaghetti Bolognese and pizza are not Venetian specialities, and when all three appear on a menu, avoid that tourist trap. On the other hand, authentic Venetian dishes may taste vaguely Turkish or Greek rather than strictly Italian, reflecting Venice's preferred trading partners for over a millennium.

☑ **Top Tip**

▶ Making yourself understood is easy if you're vegetarian or vegan – just say *'Sono vegetariano/a'* (m/f) or *'Sono vegano/a'* (m/f). Finding inspired menu options can be tricky; we've listed the best bets in this section.

ARROTOLATA
SOPPRESSA
MOZZARELLA
RUCOLA
€ 3.50

Lunch wraps for sale

Venetian Cuisine

A Beccafico All-star Italian coastal cuisine, featuring Venetian lagoon seafood, Sardinian specialities and Sicilian zing. (p38)

Anice Stellato Venice redefines the neighbourhood bistro with sustainable seafood, canalside location and spice-route flair. (p98)

Osteria alla Staffa Artistically inclined Venetian cuisine, inspired by Rialto-fresh fish, organic ingredients and artisan cheeses. (p112)

Antiche Carampane Decadent Venetian pastas and legendary *crudi* (Venetian-style sushi) in a shady courtesans' courtyard. (p80)

Al Pesador Housemade pastas and *cicheti* so creative that they rival the waterfront views along the Grand Canal. (p81)

Cicheti

All'Arco *Panini* are decoys for day-trippers; stick around and let Venice's *cicheti maestri* ply you with Rialto market–inspired fantasias. (p140)

ProntoPesce Seafood salads, soups and *crostini* (toast) don't get any fresher – this *cicheti* counter faces the Pescaria. (p81)

Dai Zemei *Crostini* with fresh twists: wild leeks, red rocket and fresh mint. (p81)

Osteria Alla Vedova Upholds hallowed Venetian happy-hour traditions, including meaty €1 *polpette* (meatballs) and dainty *ombre* (glasses of wine). (p95)

Bacaro Da Fiore Hidden in upmarket, touristy San Marco are affordable wines and authentic *cicheti*, including Venetian tripe. (p39)

Vegetarian

Le Spighe Organic vegetarian and vegan-friendly. (p114)

Osteria La Zucca Vegetarian-friendly *osteria* (tavern) championing local produce. (p81)

Tearoom Caffe Orientale Mostly vegetarian fare alongside cakes, pastries and, of course, tea. (p85)

Best
Drinking

When the siren sounds for *acqua alta* (high water), Venetians dutifully close up shop and head home to raise flood barriers – then pull on their boots and head right back out again. Why let floods disrupt happy hour? It's not just a turn of phrase: come hell or high water, Venetians will raise a toast to *la bea vita* (the good life).

Enoteche (Wine Bars)

I Rusteghi Gondoliers sing gratis after fourth-generation sommelier Giovanni d'Este's pairings of cult wines with boar salami. (p138)

Al Prosecco Organic grapes, wild-yeast fermentation, biodynamic methods: with Italy's finest natural-process wines, toasts come naturally. (p83)

Al Mercà Top-notch DOC wines, cheeses and *cicheti* enjoyed by the Grand Canal docks. (p83)

Cantina di Millevini Rivers of new and unusual Veneto vintages, poured by the glass. (p55)

Signature Cocktails

Bar Terazza Danieli Sunset-tinted Danieli, with top-shelf gin, blood-orange and apricot nectar. (p114)

Il Caffe Rosso The definitive happy-hour *spritz*: prosecco and bitters, repeat. (p55)

Locanda Cipriani Original-recipe white-peach bellinis in a rose garden. (p133)

La Serra Get fresh over pear bellinis in Napoleon's greenhouse. (p142)

Hot Drinks

VizioVirtu Artisan cocoa oozes molten hot from the copper-topped fountain. (p88)

Torrefazione Marchi *Noxea*: espresso roasted with hazelnuts right behind the marble bar. (p102)

Tearoom Caffe Orientale Bergamot-scented black tea along a quiet canal on the spice route's west end. (p85)

Caffè Lavena Proper €1 espresso served scorching at Piazza San Marco's baroque bar. (p32)

Best
For Kids

Adults think Venice is for them, but kids know better. This is where every fairy tale comes to life, where prisoners escape through the roof of a pink palace, Murano glass-blowers breathe life into pocket-sized sea dragons, and Pescaria fish balance on their tails as though spellbound. Top that, JK Rowling.

BRIAN DOBEN / GETTY IMAGES ©

Activities

Palazzo Ducale Escape from prison on the *Itinerari Segreti* (Secret Passages) tour. (p28)

Museo di Storia Naturale Discover dinosaurs, mummies and adventures on the high seas. (p78)

Lido Beaches Sculpt Venetian Gothic sand castles in gentle waves May to September. (p129)

Gilberto Penzo Build bathtub-size gondolas from kits. (p87)

Giardini Pubblici Rule the swings and slides in Napoleon's garden playground. (p110)

Row Venice Hop on the *poppa* (stern) and learn to row as gondoliers do. (p135)

Treats & Bribes

VizioVirtù Artisan chocolate everything – mousse, ice cream and truffles. (p88)

Tearoom Caffè Orientale Canalside tea parties with just-baked cakes. (p85)

Alaska Gelateria Organic gelato in classic and wild flavours, from Sicilian strawberry to island artichoke. (p81)

Le Botteghe della Solidarietà Recycled-tin Vespas, cooperative-

☑ **Top Tips**

▶ Babysitting is available at several hotels and B&Bs.

▶ Bring your own stroller.

▶ Nappies (diapers) and formula are available at groceries and pharmacies citywide.

made footballs and fairtrade chocolates. (p47)

Best
Museums

Peek inside Grand Canal palaces donated to Venice, and you'll find they're packed to attic rafters with Prada couture, samurai armour and the odd dinosaur. Though he tried for 11 years, Napoleon couldn't steal all the treasures Venetians had hoarded for centuries. Generous benefactors have restored Venice's treasure-box museums and added plenty to them, too.

Venetian All-Star Showcases

Gallerie dell'Accademia Watch Venetian painters set the world ablaze with saturated colour and censorship-defying art. (p50)

Ca' Rezzonico The sun seems to shine inside baroque Ca' Rezzonico, from Tieopolo's salon ceilings to the Vedutisti (Landscape) gallery. (p58)

Palazzo Ducale The doge's home decor is the world's prettiest propaganda, featuring Veronese, Tintoretto, Tiepolo and Titian. (p28)

Museo Correr Palace rooms dedicated to pink bellinis and blood-red Carpaccios, plus philosophers by Veronese, Titian and Tintoretto in the library. (p36)

I Frari Titian's glowing Madonna outshines even Canova, Bellini and Longhena. (p71)

Scuola Grande di San Rocco Tintoretto upstages Veronese with action-packed scenes of angelic rescue squads. (p68)

Fashion-Forward Palaces

Museo Fortuny The radical fashion-house that freed women from corsets keeps raising eyebrows. (p36)

Fondazione Prada Futurist suits, video art and Duchamp suitcases are making waves along the Grand Canal inside stately Renaissance palace Ca' Corner. (p78)

Palazzo Mocenigo Find fashion inspiration in this palace packed with Venetian glamour. (p79)

Modern Art Museums

Peggy Guggenheim Collection Pollock, Rothko, Kandinsky and company make a mighty splash on the Grand Canal. (p52)

Palazzo Grassi Murakami's manic daisies, Kruger's ominous slogans and other provocations in a Grand Canal palace. (p36)

Punta della Dogana Mega-installations are docked inside Venice's customs warehouses. (p58)

Ca' Pesaro Klimts, Kandinskys and other modern masterpieces Venice slyly snapped up at the Biennale. (p78)

Best
Venetian
Innovations

FRANK FELL / GETTY IMAGES ©

The city built on water was never afraid to attempt the impossible. When plague struck, Venice set global quarantine standards. Under attack by Genoa, Venice's Arsenale churned out a warship a day on the world's first assembly line. After losing its shipping fortune, Venice sang for its supper, innovating modern opera.

Venetian Inventions

Basilica di Santa Maria della Salute A tribute to plague survival, aided by a Venetian innovation: quarantine. (p58)

Squero San Trovaso Watch Venice's signature ride – the gondola – being hand-shaped at this shipyard. (p60)

Ottica Carraro Eyeglasses were invented in Venice, and you can still get your own made-in-Venice pair here. (p45)

Museo Fortuny See how women cut loose from corseted convention c 1907. (p36)

Palazzo Mocenigo Venetian courtesans set the fashion for platform shoes; even Lady Gaga would stumble in the 17th-century elephant shoes in this permanent collection. (p79)

Historical Hot Spots

Arsenale Venice's legendary shipyards built a warship in a day on the world's first assembly line. (p111)

Magazzini del Sale Venice's salt monopoly funded hospices, architectural wonders and Italy's age of exploration. (p60)

The Ghetto The Jewish island community defied Inquisition orders, and sparked a Renaissance. (p92)

Teatro La Fenice Modern opera emerged in a blaze of glory from Venice's public opera house. (p43)

Torre dell'Orologio From atop this medieval timepiece, Filippo Tommaso Marinetti threw his Futurist manifesto for machine-age modernism. (p36)

La Pietà Orphan orchestras performed benefit concerts of original works by baroque composer and musical director Antonio Vivaldi. (p116)

Best
Architecture

From glittering Byzantine churches to post-modern palaces, Venice astonishes at every gondola turn. Its 1000-year architectural history has several high-water marks: pointy Venetian Gothic arches rounded off in the Renaissance; Palladio-revived rigorous classicism amid baroque flourishes; and stark modernism relaxing around decadent Lido Liberty (art nouveau). Now that the latest architectural trend is creative repurposing, it's all making a comeback.

Renovations in Progress

After a disastrous flood hit Venice in 1966, architecture aficionados worldwide aided Venetians in bailing out *palazzi* and reinforcing foundations. With the support of Unesco and funding from 24 affiliated organisations worldwide, Venice has completed 1500 restoration projects in 40 years.

Today the city balances preservation and modern living, though controversies remain. Plans to transform drab Marco Polo Airport with Frank Gehry's €80 million Venice Gateway complex remain stalled, and Italy's Culture Ministry requires revisions to Rem Koolhaas' 2012 designs for a Benetton complex on the Grand Canal. Yet there's more modern architecture here than you might think: one-third of all buildings in Venice have been raised since 1919.

Pleasure Palaces

Ca' d'Oro The grandest palace on the Grand Canal, with Venetian Gothic trilobate (three-lobed) arches and tiara-like crennalation. (p98)

Palazzo Ducale Don't been fooled by Antonio da Ponte's pretty pink Gothic loggia: this palace means business. (p28)

Ca' Rezzonico Renaissance grandeur gone baroque: designed by Longhena, finished by Massari and crowned with Tiepolo ceilings. (p58)

Palazzo Grassi Gae Aulenti and Tadao Ando peeled back rococo flourishes to reveal Giorgio Massari's neoclassical lines. (p36)

Palazzo Querini Stampalia Baroque beauty with high-modernist

Grand Canal (p86)

updates: Carlo Scarpa–designed gardens and gates, Mario Botta library and cafe. (p110)

Grand Hotel Excelsior
Giovanni Sardi's decadent Byzantine-Moorish beach resort, built 1898–1908 with Fortuny *stile liberty* (art-nouveau) interiors. (p133)

Divine Architecture

Basilica di San Marco
Byzantine domes glimmer with golden mosaics. (p24)

Basilica di Santa Maria della Salute Longhena's bubble-domed marvel, believed to have mystical curative powers. (p58)

Chiesa di San Giorgio Maggiore Palladio's expansive, effortlessly uplifting church and cloisters. (p120)

Chiesa di Santa Maria dei Miracoli The Lombardos' little Renaissance miracle in polychrome marble. (p98)

Schola Spagnola The theatrical, elliptical women's gallery attributed to Longhena. (p93)

Modern Marvels

Biennale pavilions
High-modernist pavilion architecture, which often steals the show at Art Biennales. (p110)

Punta della Dogana
Customs warehouses creatively repurposed into cutting-edge installation-art galleries by Tadao Ando. (p58)

Negozio Olivetti
Forward-thinking Carlo Scarpa transformed a dusty souvenir shop into a high-tech showcase c 1958. (p37)

Fondazione Giorgio Cini Former naval academy rocks the boat as an avant-garde art gallery. (p121)

Best
Art

Water may be the first thing you notice about Venice when you arrive, but as you get closer, you'll discover that this city is actually saturated with art. Canals are just brief interruptions between artworks in this Unesco World Heritage site, with more art treasures than any other city. Through censorship, plague and nonstop parties, Venice kept creating masterpieces.

Venetian Masterpieces

Gallerie dell'Accademia Veronese's triumph over censorship: *Feast in the House of Levi*. (p50)

I Frari Titian's red-hot Madonna altarpiece: *Assunta*. (p70)

Scuola Grande di San Rocco Tintoretto to the rescue: *St Mark in Glory*. (p68)

Ca' Rezzonico Longhi's naughty socialites and their disapproving dogs: Salon Pietro Longhi. (p58)

Palazzo Ducale Tiepolo's Venice is a lion-taming blonde: *Receiving the Gifts of the Sea from Neptune*. (p28)

Modern Showcases

Biennale The world's most prestigious visual-art showcase, held in even-numbered years. (p113)

Fondazione Giorgio Cini Peter Greenaway videos in Palladio cloisters and blockbuster shows in a naval academy. (p121)

Punta della Dogana Historical customs warehouses retrofitted for the future with installation art. (p58)

Magazzini del Sale Rotating exhibits powered by robots. (p60)

☑ **Top Tip**

▶ See more art for less: get the 16-church Chorus Pass (p166), the combined 72-hour ticket to Punta Della Dogana and Palazzo Grassi, or the Civic Museum Pass (p166), which covers entry to 11 museums.

Best
For Romance

Traffic never seemed so romantic as at sunset in Venice, when arias echo under the Ponte dei Sospiri (Bridge of Sighs) from passing gondolas. Venice is purpose-built for romance, with slow boats and opera instead of honking cars and curses. You don't have to be Casanova – Venice makes every romantic gesture grand.

Date-Night Dining

Osteria Boccadoro Sensational seafood and chocolate mousse for two in a secluded *campo*. (p100)

Al Covo Share plates in a cosy, wood-beamed trattoria. (p112)

I Figli delle Stelle Jazz nights, decadent pasta and canalfront dining. (p127)

A Beccafico Spirited seafood and a staggering wine list in a picturesque piazza. (p38)

Trattoria Corte Sconta A secret garden getaway with Rialto Market– inspired daily menus. (p114)

Romantic Gestures

Palazetto Bru Zane Lingering glances at concerts in a frescoed pleasure palace. (p85)

Teatro La Fenice Welling up at opera premieres. (p43)

Caffè Florian Sunset tango across Piazza San Marco. (p33)

Palazzo Contarini del Bovolo Clandestine smooches in a hidden Renaissance courtyard. (p38)

Bauer Palladio Spa Massages and rose-petal baths in Palladian splendour. (p131)

Gondola A proposal… or at least a compelling proposition.

☑ **Top Tips**

▸ Plan romantic getaways in winter, when you'll have the best bistros to yourselves.

▸ Book tickets to opera premieres and weekend concerts well ahead.

▸ Need someplace special for a *prosecco* toast or proposal? Ask a gondolier – they're experts.

SERGIO PITAMITZ / GETTY IMAGES ©

Best
Shopping

Your Venice souvenirs may be hard to describe back home without sounding like you're bragging. 'It's an original', you'll say, 'and I met the artisan.' From hypnotic marble-paper handbags to glass-dragon goblets, Venice's artisan originals are surprisingly affordable, and your purchase rewards the delicate handling and enduring imagination of Venice's artisans.

Venetian Home Decor

ElleElle Murano art glass balancing modernity and tradition, with essential shapes and dramatic colours. (p125)

Chiarastella Cattana Locally loomed linens as plush as velvet, in history-inspired modern designs and Venetian colours. (p45)

Fortuny Tessuti Artistici Hand-printed, Bohemian chic cotton for cushions, curtains and walls. (p126)

Cartavenezia Roaring lion reliefs and free-form lampshades, all in sculpted paper. (p88)

Danghyra Hand-thrown minimalist porcelain with a Venetian shock of colour. (p64)

☑ Top Tips

▶ Shelves of delicate handicrafts may be labelled *non toccare* (don't touch); ask to see a piece.

▶ Open-air markets held March to October and around Christmas; upcoming dates are listed at www.turismo venezia.it (search for markets).

▶ Murano glass isn't necessarily less expensive in Murano than in Venice proper, but Murano's art-glass selection is dazzling.

Shopping on Ponte di Rialto (p73)

Venetian Fashion Statements

Fiorella Gallery Subversive Venetian rocker chic, including lilac, silk-velvet smoking jackets hand-printed with red rats. (p45)

Marina e Susanna Sent Minimalist Murano glass jewellery with vivid colours and architectural impact. (p64)

Cárte Marbled endpaper breaks free of books and turns into handbags, cocktail rings and jewellery boxes. (p74)

Godi Fiorenza London-trained Venetian sisters design avant-garde ensembles inspired by divas and teddy bears. (p45)

Sigfrido Cipolato Exquisite enamelled diadems and skull rings. (p116)

Banco Lotto 10 Diva-worthy opera wraps made by a women's prison collective. (p117)

Giovanna Zanella Hand-sculpted custom footwear by Venice's most imaginative artisan shoemaker. (p117)

Pied à Terre *Furlane* (gondolier shoes) in vibrant colours and luxe fabrics. (p75)

Only-in-Venice Gifts

Gilberto Penzo Scale-model gondole. (p87)

I Vetri a Lume di Amadi Glass mosquitoes. (p88)

Gianni Basso Calling cards with the lion of San Marco. (p104)

Malefatte Slick man-bags made from vinyl art-museum-show banners by a Venetian prison cooperative. (p45)

Best
Entertainment

Since the fall of its shipping empire, Venice has lived by its wits. No one throws a party like Venice, from Carnevale masquerades to Regata Storica floating parades – plus live opera, baroque music and jazz year-round, and summer movie premieres and beach concerts.

Festivals

If you'd survived the plague and Austrian invasion, you'd throw parties too – Venice celebrates with November's Festa della Madonna della Salute and July's Festa del Redentore (see www.turismo venezia.it). Regatta season from May's Vogalonga (www.vogalonga.com) to September's Regata Storica (www.regatastoricavenezia.it) sees cheering crowds along canalbanks.

The Venice International Film Festival rolls out its red carpet from the last weekend in August through the first week of September, bringing together international star power and Italian fashion.

Carnevale brings partying masqueraders onto the streets for two weeks preceding Lent. Tickets to La Fenice's masked balls run up to €230, but there are public costume parties in every *campo* (square) and a Grand Canal flotilla to mark the end.

Live Music & Opera

A magnet for music fans for four centuries, Venice supplies a soundtrack of opera, classical music and jazz. You can still enjoy music as Venetians did centuries ago: Teatro La Fenice (p43) has been one of the world's top opera houses since 1792, while historical La Pietà (p116) orphanage is the original Vivaldi venue. Due to noise regulations in this small city with big echoes, shows typically end by 11pm.

☑ **Top Tips**

▶ For upcoming openings, concerts, performances and other events, check listings at www .veneziadavivere .com and www .turismovenezia.it.

▶ Purchase tickets in advance at the venue website, www.venice connected.com, www.musicinvenice .com, or from **HelloVenezia ticket outlets** (☎ 041 24 24; www.hellovenezia.it).

▶ For performance schedules, online ticket sales and concert gift cards, see www.musicinvenice .com.

Teatro La Fenice (p43)

Events

Venice Biennale (June to November) Outlandish openings in pavillions tricked out like surreal doll-houses. (p113)

Venice International Film Festival (August to September; www .labiennale.org/it/ cinema) Red carpets sizzle with star power, and deserving films actually win.

Carnevale (January/February; www.carnevale .venezia.it) Party in costume until wigs itch and livers twitch (about three weeks).

Venezia Jazz Festival (July; www.venetojazz .com) Jazz greats and the odd pop star play historical venues, including Piazza San Marco.

Live Music

Teatro La Fenice Divas hit new highs in this historical jewel-box theatre for under 1000 lucky ticket-holders. (p43)

Interpreti Veneziani Venice's classical talents go for baroque in Chiesa San Vidal. (p33)

Palazzetto Bru Zane Leading interpreters of Romantic music raise the Sebastiano Ricci–frescoed roof. (p85)

Musica a Palazzo Operatic dramas unfold in a Grand Canal palace, from receiving-room overtures to bedroom grand finales. (p33)

Caffè Florian Without nimble accompaniment from Florian's orchestra, the sun might not be allowed to set in Piazza San Marco. (p33)

Palazzo Querini Stampalia Weekend chamber-music concerts in silk-clad salons. (p110)

Summer Spots

Summer Arena Before Venice International Film Festival starts up, free movies and theatre illuminate nights in Campo San Polo – visit www .comune.venezia.it for schedules. (p85)

B.each On the Lido, check out free summer cinema, beach concerts and club nights. (p129)

Blue Moon This Lido beach complex hosts concerts and club nights in summer. (p129)

Best
Secrets

Yellow signs across Venice helpfully point out major routes to San Marco, Rialto and Ferrovia (train station). But here's the secret to any great Venetian adventure: ignore those signs. Venice's finest moments are hidden in crooked *calli* (lanes), shady *cortili* (courtyards) and *palazzo* (palace) attics. Look no further for Venice's best artisans' studios, finest seafood, spy headquarters and walk-in ball-gown closets.

Freebies

Despite its centuries-old reputation as a playground for Europe's elite, Venice's finest moments are freebies. Golden glimpses of heaven in Basilica di San Marco are gratis, and the diocese offers free guided mosaic tours. Entry is free and potentially curative at Basilica di Santa Maria della Salute, built as thanks for Venice's salvation from the plague, with a dome said to radiate healing energy. Carnevale is best celebrated in the streets – especially on the first night, when wine fountains flow free along the Grand Canal.

Hidden Wonders

Chiesa di San Francesco della Vigna All-star Venetian art showcase and Palladio's first commission, down by Castello's boatyard docks. (p110)

Chiesa di Santa Maria dei Miracoli The little neighbourhood church with big Renaissance ideas and priceless marble, amid a maze of canals. (p98)

Museo di Storia Naturale Dinosaurs, mummies and other bizarre scientific specimens brought home by intrepid Venetian explorers – all inside a Turkish fortress. (p78)

Cattedrale di Santa Maria Assunta Lambs bleat encouragement as you walk through this overgrown island

View from Basilica di San Marco's *campanile* (bell tower) (p38)

towards golden glory in apse mosaics. (p122)

Ghetto synagogues Climb to rooftop synagogues on tours run by Museo Ebraico. (p93)

Palazzo Contarini del Bovolo A secret spiral staircase in an ancient hidden courtyard sets the scene for a clandestine smooch. (p38)

Trade Secrets Revealed

Museo del Vetro Murano kept master glass-making techniques under wraps for centuries, but here they're on full display. (p125)

Arsenale Workers at Venice's legendary shipyards were sworn to secrecy, but now you can see how they built a ship a day. (p111)

Museo del Merletto Watch lace artisans tat traditional Venetian patterns handed down through centuries. (p132)

Museo Storico Navale Bodyguards wouldn't let anyone near the *bucintoro* (ducal barge), until now. (p112)

Row Venice Learn to row across lagoon waters standing, like gondolieri do, from regatta champ Jane Caporal. (p135)

Mysteries in the Attic

Palazzo Mocenigo Head up to the attic closet to discover the kind of shoes a Venetian courtesan wore for streetwalking. (p79)

Palazzo Ducale A tour of the attic prison will reveal just how Casanova escaped prison while the doge slept downstairs. (p28)

Torre dell'Orologio A tower-top tour will give an up-close look at those bronze bell-ringers who moon Basilica di San Marco at midnight. (p36)

Best
Island Escapes

MICHAEL SICK / GETTY IMAGES ©

Drift away on the blue lagoon, and you never know where you'll end up next: at a fiery glass-blowing furnace, an organic farmer's market at an island prison, an orphanage designed by Palladio that's now a luxury spa. Venice's lagoon offers not only idyllic island retreats – beach clubs, vineyard lunches and farm stays – but also outlandish escapes from reality.

Destination Dining

Terra e Acqua Fish stew aboard a Venetian barge. (p135)

Venissa Ultramodern, ultralocal seafood in an island vineyard. (p132)

Le Garzette Farm-to-table dining hidden between Lido beaches. (p132)

I Figli delle Stelle Jazz trios and scenic seafood pasta along Giudecca Canal. (p127)

Acquastanca Baked goods wedged between glass-blowing studios. (p132)

Outdoor Attractions

Lido Beaches When temperatures nudge past 29°C, Venice races to the Lido-bound *vaporetto*

(passenger ferry) to claim sandy beachfront. (p129)

Torcello Rare lagoon birds swoop lazily past the Byzantine campanile on this wild island, no longer stalked by Hemingway. (p122)

Burano The vibrant colour-blocked fishing village is a photographer's dream. (p132)

Organic Farmers Market Produce fresh from the island prison sells every Thursday on Giudecca. (p127)

Vogalonga The regatta race is a fine excuse to laze around Mazzorbo, raising toasts to rowers' health. (p132)

Row Venice Row to picnics on Venice's island cemetery. (p135)

☑ **Top Tips**

▸ Outer islands are blissfully peaceful in the October-to-April off-season, though many restaurants and shops close.

▸ Ask locals to point out favourite lagoon shorebirds, including white ibis, purple heron and cormorants.

▸ Please pick up after island picnics to protect Venice's fragile ecosystem.

Fondazione Giorgio Cini Explore the new Borges Labyrinth behind Palladio's cloisters on Isola di San Michele. (p121)

Survival Guide

Survival Guide

Before You Go

When to Go

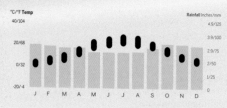

→ **Winter (Nov-Feb)**
Chilly, serene days and sociable nights, especially during Carnevale.

→ **Spring (Mar-May)**
Bring umbrellas and enjoy sublime seafood, easy conversation and bargain rates – except around Easter.

→ **Summer (Jun-Aug)**
Biennales and Lido beaches maximise hot summer days. Crowds thin and rates drop July to August, when some businesses close.

→ **Autumn (Sep-Nov)**
After Venice Film Festival, crowds retreat and Venetians come out to play on warm days.

Book Your Stay

☑ **Top Tip** Rates double during peak times: Christmas through New Year, Carnevale, Easter week, Biennale launches (June) and Venice Film Festival (August to September).

→ Book ahead for weekend getaways and high-season visits.

→ Check individual hotel websites for online deals.

→ Confirm arrival at least 72 hours in advance, or hotels may assume you've changed plans.

→ For low-season savings of 40% or more, plan visits for November, early December or January to March (except Carnevale. Deals may be found July to August.

Useful Websites

APT (www.turismo venezia.it) Lists licensed B&Bs and rental apartments in Venice proper.

artmentsApart (www
artmentsapart.com)
ats for rent by the day.

B Planet (www.bb
anet.com) Search Ven-
 B&Bs and apartment
ntals by area, price
nge and availability.

nely Planet (www
nelyplanet.com) Expert
uthor reviews, user feed-
ck and booking engine.

**nice Apartment
ental** (www.veniceapart-
ent.com) Apartments
 daily or weekly rental.

st Budget

o & Gio (www.giogio
nice.com) Modern
roque B&B near Piazza
n Marco.

resteria Valdese
ww.foresteriavenezia.
 Historical, frescoed
stel near Zanipolo.

lo Squero (www.allos-
uero.it) Garden retreat
 a converted shipyard.

ocanda Sant'Anna
ww.locandasantanna
m) Spacious, antique-
ed rooms off quiet
astello *campo* (piazza).

otel Ai Do Mori (www
otelaidomori.com)
nug wood-beamed
uestrooms behind
asilica di San Marco.

Ostello Venezia (www.
ostellovenezia
.it) Restored hostel on
Giudecca Canal.

Best Midrange

Ca' Zanardi (www
.cazanardi.eu) Cannar-
egio 16th-century palace
rooms with original
fittings.

Novecento (www
.novecento.biz) Bohemi-
an chic B&B near Campo
Santo Stefano.

Hotel Le Isole
(www.hotel-leisole.it)
Courtyard hotel near
Piazza San Marco, with
lavish breakfasts.

Palazzo Schiavoni
(www.palazzoschiavoni
.com) Frescoed boutique
hotel in a Castello palace.

Al Redentore di Venezia
(www.alredentoredivne-
ezia.com) Sleek serviced
apartments on Giudecca.

Oltre Il Giardino (www
.oltreilgiardino-venezia.
com) Designer glam gar-
den B&B near I Frari.

Best Top-End

Palazzo Abadessa (www
.abadessa.com) Opulent
B&B in a 1540 palace
near Ponte di Rialto
(Rialto bridge).

Gritti Palace (www
.hotelgrittipalacevenice
.com) Fully restored
historical Grand Canal
luxury hotel.

Aqua Palace (www
.aquapalace.it) Romantic,
aristocratic hotel on a
quiet San Marco canal.

**Bauer Palladio Hotel &
Spa** (www.palladiohotel
spa.com) Palladio cloister
converted into serene
Giudecca spa-hotel.

Arriving
in Venice

☑ **Top Tip** For the best
way to get to your accom-
modation, see p17.

From Marco
Polo Airport

**Vaporetto
(Passenger Ferry)**
Alilaguna operates ferry
services (€15) to Venice
from the airport ferry
dock (an eight-minute
walk from the terminal);
rides take 45 to 90
minutes to reach most
destinations.

Linea Blu (Blue Line) Stops include Lido, San Marco and Dorsoduro

Linea Rossa (Red Line) Stops at Murano and Lido.

Linea Arancia (Orange Line) Stops at Stazione Santa Lucia, Rialto and San Marco via the Grand Canal.

Linea Gialla (Yellow Line) Stops at Murano and Fondamenta Nuove (Cannaregio).

Bus

Piazzale Roma is the only point within central Venice accessible by bus. *Vaporetto* lines and water taxis depart from Piazzale Roma docks.

➡ **ATVO** (Azienda Trasporti Veneto Orientale; ☎ 0421 59 46 71; www.atvo.it) Buses depart from the airport terminal to Venice's Piazzale Roma (€6, about 30 minutes, every 30 minutes 8am to midnight).

➡ **ACTV** (Azienda del Consorzio Trasporti Veneziano; ☎ 041 24 24; www.actv.it) Bus 5 departs the airport terminal to Piazzale Roma (€6, about one hour, four per hour).

Water Taxi

Water taxis depart airport docks and cost €90 to €110 to Venice, or €32 per person for shared taxis (eight passengers with 10 bags maximum).

Car

Cars cannot be taken into central Venice. At Piazzale Roma and Tronchetto parking garages, expect to pay €21 or more for every 24 hours.

➡ From Piazzale Roma docks, you can take a *vaporetto* or water taxi.

➡ **People Mover monorail** (APM; www.apmvenezia.com; per ride €1; ⏰7am-11pm Mon-Sat, 8am-9pm Sun) Connects Tronchetto garage with Piazzale Roma. Ferry 17 transports vehicles from Tronchetto to the Lido, where cars are allowed.

From Stazione Santa Lucia

Vaporetto

Several *vaporetto* lines depart Ferrovia (train station) docks:

Line 1 Covers the Grand Canal to San Marco and Lido every 10 minutes.

Line 2 Covers the Grand Canal with fewer stops, returning via Giudecca.

Lines 41, 42 Circles Venice's outer perimeter.

Lines 51, 52 Covers the 41/42 route plus Lido, with fewer stops.

Line N All-night local service stops along Giudecca, the Grand Canal, San Marco and Lido (every 40 minutes, 11.30pm to 4am).

Water Taxi

The water-taxi stand is at the station dock; fares start at €8.90 and add up quickly at €1.80/minute.

Getting Around

On Foot

☑ **Best for...** shortcuts and getting around San Marco, San Polo and Santa Croce.

➡ Walking in Venice requires comfortable shoes with good tread for footbridges and slippery canalbanks. Gumboots may be handy November to March.

➡ Running is limited to less-travelled routes in

e Giardini and along
rsoduro's waterfront.

aporetto

 Best for... island-
pping, traveling with
ildren and/or baggage,
d reaching far-flung
stinations.

ACTV operates Venice's
enic but slow vaporetto,
e public passenger
rry service.

HelloVenezia (www.hello
nezia.com) sells tickets
d passes and posts
stem maps at dockside
ket booths and online.

Major stops often have
o separate docks serv-
g the same vaporetto
e, heading in opposite
rections. Check landing
ck signs to make sure
u're at the right dock
r the direction you
ant.

Vaporetto lines are
ost crowded from 8am
10am and 6pm to 8pm,
hen some lines make
ly limited stops.

Some lines stop run-
ng by around 9pm.
he N offers all-night
cal service covering
udecca, the Grand Ca-
al, San Marco and Lido
1.30pm to 4am, about
ery 40 minutes).

Tickets & Passes

➜ Single vaporetto rides
cost €7; for frequent
vaporetto use, get a
timed pass for unlim-
ited travel within a set
period (12-/24-/36-/48-
/72-hour passes cost
€18/20/25/30/35).

➜ Visitors aged 14-29
can get a three-day
vaporetto ticket for €18
(ID required).

➜ Always validate your
ticket at yellow dockside
machines at first usage.
If you're caught without
a valid ticket, you'll be
subject to a €60 fine.

Gondola

☑ **Best for** ... romance
and canal photo-ops.

➜ Rates run €80 per 40
minutes (six passengers
maximum) daytime or
€100 per 40 minutes
7pm to 8am, not includ-
ing songs (negotiated
separately) or tips. Ad-
ditional time is charged
in 20-minute increments
(day/night €40/50).

➜ Gondolas cluster at
stazi (stops) along the
Grand Canal (ie Ferrovia
and Rialto) and near
major monuments (ie I
Frari and Basilica di San
Marco).

➜ Call the citywide gon-
dola pick-up service on
☎041 528 50 75 for pick-
up at a convenient canal.

Traghetto

A traghetto is the public
gondola service locals use
to cross the Grand Canal
between bridges (€0.50,
9am to 6pm, some routes
9am to noon).

Water Taxi

☑ **Best for...** late-night
or early-morning arrivals
and departures, especially
with baggage or for large
groups.

➜ Licensed water taxis
offer stylish transport
in sleek teak boats, but
it'll cost you €8.90 plus
€1.80 per minute, plus €6
for hotel service and extra
for 10pm to 7am service,
luggage and large groups.

➜ Ask your accommoda-
tion to book for you – you
may be able to share a
taxi with other guests
headed to the airport – or
call a citywide service line
directly on ☎041 522 23
03 or ☎041 240 67 11.

➜ Even if you're in a hurry,
don't encourage your taxi
driver to speed through
Venice: motoschiaffi (mo-
torboat wakes) expose
Venice's ancient founda-
tions to degradation.

Bicycle

☑ **Best for...**
exploring the Lido.

Cycling is banned in central Venice. Bicycle-hire places cluster around the Lido *vaporetto* stop, including **Lido on Bike** (☏041 526 80 19; www .lidoonbike.it; Gran Viale 21b; bikes per 90min/day €5/9; ⏱9am-7pm Apr-Sep); ID is required.

Essential Information

Business Hours

Exceptions to the following hours are noted in listings.

Banks 8.30am to 1.30pm and 3.30pm to 5.30pm Monday to Friday; some open Saturday mornings.

Restaurants Noon to 2.30pm and 7pm to 10pm.

Shops 10am to 1pm and 3.30pm to 7pm (or 4pm or 7.30pm) Monday to Saturday. Most Murano glass showrooms close by 6pm.

Discount Cards

Includes single entry to Palazzo Ducale, 10 Civic Museums, 16 Chorus churches, Palazzo Querini Stampalia and Museo Ebraico; two free toilet passes; discounted entry to additional museums (eg Museo Fortuny & Peggy Guggenheim Collection). **Venice Card** (www.venicecard.com; adult/youth €39.90/29.90) is valid for seven days. Purchase at participating museums or tourist office.

Chorus Pass

Covers single entry to 16 major churches (€10; www.chorusvenezia.org). Valid for one year. Buy at participating churches.

Civic Museum Pass

This **pass** (www.visitmuve .it; adult/reduced €20/14) covers single entry to 11 Civic Museums, including Palazzo Ducale & Museo Correr. Valid for six months. Buy at participating museums or tourist office.

Museum Card

This **pass** (www.visitmuve.it; adult/reduced €20/14) covers Palazzo Ducale and Museo Correr. Purchase at either location.

Electricity

230V/50Hz

Emergency

Ospedale Civile (☏041 529 41 11; Campo SS Giovan e Paolo 6777) Venice's ma

spital; for emergency
re and dental treat-
ent, ask for *pronto
ccorso* (casualty).

oney

edit cards Accepted at
ost hotels, some shops
d restaurants.

oney changers At
nks, airport and some
tels; official rates at
ww.xe.com.

pping Ten per cent
tional for good restau-
nt, hotel and gondola
rvices.

avellers cheques
avelex is at the airport
d Piazza San Marco
2 (☑041 528 73 58).

ublic Holidays

olidays that may affect
ening hours and transit
hedules include:

**apodanno/Anno
uovo** (New Year's Day)
January

pifania/Befana
piphany) 6 January

nedí dell'Angelo
ood Friday) March/
ril

**asquetta/Lunedí
ell'Angelo** (Easter Mon-
ay) March/April

Dos & Don'ts

➡ Do keep right along narrow lanes to let people
pass on the left.

➡ Do offer help to people struggling with strollers
or bags on bridges.

➡ Do say hello before you ask for directions;
everyone gets lost in Venice, so don't panic, and
be polite.

➡ Don't season before you taste: Venetians be-
lieve fresh seafood doesn't need camouflage like
lemon, mustard, parmesan or hot pepper.

**Giorno della Liberazi-
one** (Liberation Day) 25
April

Festa del Lavoro
(Labour Day) 1 May

Festa della Repubblica
(Republic Day) 2 June

Ferragosto (Feast of the
Assumption) 15 August

Ognissanti (All Saints'
Day) 1 November

Immaculata Concezione
(Feast of the Immaculate
Conception) 8 December

Natale (Christmas Day)
25 December

Festa di Santo Stefano
(Boxing Day) 26
December

Safe Travel

➡ **Precautions** Crime
rates are low in Venice,

but keep valuables secure
in crowds.

➡ **Children** Some historical Venice accommoda-
tions, sights and boats
are not child-safe; check
age requirements and
inquire before reserving.

➡ **Rising water** See the
Acqua Alta box (p104).

Telephone

Mobile Phones

GSM and tri-band mobile
phones can be used
in Venice with a local
SIM card (available at
telephone and electron-
ics stores).

Phone Codes

➡ Italy country code:
☑39

➡ Venice City Code:
☑041 (land lines only)

Making International and Domestic Calls

International calls from Italy Dial ☎00, then country code, area code and telephone number.

Calling Venice from abroad Dial the international access number, then ☎39 (Italy's country code), then ☎041 (Venice city code), then the telephone number.

Domestic calls Dial the city code then phone number.

Domestic calls to Italian mobile phones Dial the three-digit mobile prefix, then phone number (no city code needed).

International calls to Italian mobiles Dial the international access number, then ☎39, then the three-digit mobile prefix, then phone number.

Toilets

Public toilets Available near tourist attractions (€1.50, 7am to 7pm).

Bars and cafes For customers only.

Museums This is your best option – where available.

Tourist Information

Azienda di Promozione Turistica (☎041 529 87 11; www.turismovenezia .it; Piazza San Marco 71f; ◷9.45am-3.15pm Mon-Sat) Venice's tourism office provides information on events, attractions and transport.

Venezia da Vivere (www.veneziadavivere.com) Event and nightlife listings online.

Un Ospite di Venezia (A Guest in Venice; www.uno-spitedivenezia.it) A monthly event calendar available online and in hotels.

Travellers with Disabilities

➡ **Comune di Venezia** (www.comune.venezia.it) Offers an online *Accessible Venice* map (listed under 'Your Life').

➡ **Train Disabled Assistance Office** (◷7am-9pm) Located at platform 4 in Venice's Santa Lucia station.

➡ **Vaporetto** Wheelchai access and discounted fares apply (€1.30); a companion travels free charge.

Visas

Not required for EU citizens. Nationals of Australia, Brazil, Canada Japan, New Zealand and the USA do not need visas for visits up to 90 days. For more information, visit the Italian foreign ministry website (http://www.esteri.it).

Behind the Scenes

Send Us Your Feedback

We love to hear from travellers – your comments help make our books better. We read every word, and we guarantee that your feedback goes straight to the authors. Visit **lonelyplanet.com/contact** to submit your updates and suggestions.

Note: We may edit, reproduce and incorporate your comments in Lonely Planet products such as guidebooks, websites and digital products, so let us know if you don't want your comments reproduced or your name acknowledged. For a copy of our privacy policy visit lonelyplanet.com/privacy.

Our Readers

Many thanks to the travellers who used the last edition and wrote to us with helpful hints, useful advice and interesting anecdotes: Helen Carr, Elina Kuzjukevica, Marta Szabo and Gaye Tirimanne.

Alison's Thanks

Mille grazie e tanti baci alla mia famiglia a Roma and stateside, the Bings, Ferrys and Marinuccis; to editorial mastermind Joe Bindloss; and *prosecco* toasts to Venezia intelligentsia Cristina Bottero, Alberto Toso Fei, Francesca Forni, Rosanna Corrò, Giantantonio De Vincenzo, Giovanni d'Este, Francesco e Matteo Pinto, and Jane and Luigi Caporal. *Ma sopra tutto* to Marco Flavio Marinucci, for making *la bea vita* possible, even outside Venice.

Acknowledgments

Cover photograph: Grand Canal, Venice; Massimo Borchi/4Corners.

This Book

This 3rd edition of Lonely Planet's *Pocket Venice* guidebook was researched and written by Alison Bing. The previous two editions were also written by Alison Bing. This guidebook was commissioned in Lonely Planet's London office and produced by the following:

Commissioning Editors Joe Bindloss, Helena Smith
Coordinating Editors Fionnuala Twomey, Pete Cruttenden
Cartographer James Leversha
Coordinating Layout Designer Mazzy Prinsep
Managing Editor Annelies Mertens
Senior Editor Karyn Noble
Senior Cartographer Anthony Phelan

Managing Layout Designer Jane Hart
Cover Research Naomi Parker
Internal Image Research Aude Vauconsant
Thanks to Anita Banh, Laura Crawford, Ryan Evans, Larissa Frost, Genesys India, Jouve India, Asha Ioculari, Andi Jones, Trent Paton, Dianne Schallmeiner, Kerrianne Southway, Gerard Walker

Index

See also separate subindexes for:

⊗ **Eating p173**

⊖ **Drinking p173**

☺ **Entertainment p174**

🔒 **Shopping p174**

Our Writer

Alison Bing

When she's not scribbling notes in church pews or methodically eating her way across Venice's *sestieri* (neighbourhoods), Alison contributes to Lonely Planet's *Venice, USA, Morocco, San Francisco, Marrakesh, California* and *Discover Italy* guides, as well as food, art and architecture magazines. Alison holds a bachelor's degree in art history and a master's degree from the Fletcher School of Law and Diplomacy, a joint program of Tufts and Harvard Universities – perfectly respectable diplomatic credentials she regularly undermines with opinionated culture commentary for newspapers, magazines, TV and radio. Currently she divides her time between San Francisco and an Etruscan hilltop town in central Italy with partner Marco Flavio Marinucci; she tweets her finds www.twitter.com/AlisonBing.

Published by Lonely Planet Publications Pty Ltd
ABN 36 005 607 983
3rd edition – January 2014
ISBN 978 1 74220 141 2
© Lonely Planet 2014   Photographs © as indicated 2014
10 9 8 7 6 5 4 3
Printed in China

Although the authors and Lonely Planet have taken all reasonable care in preparing this book, we make no warranty about the accuracy or completeness of its content and, to the maximum extent permitted, disclaim all liability arising from its use.

All rights reserved. No part of this publication may be copied, stored in a retrieval system, or transmitted in any form by any means, electronic, mechanical, recording or otherwise, except brief extracts for the purpose of review, and no part of this publication may be sold or hired, without the written permission of the publisher. Lonely Planet and the Lonely Planet logo are trademarks of Lonely Planet and are registered in the US Patent and Trademark Office and in other countries. Lonely Planet does not allow its name or logo to be appropriated by commercial establishments, such as retailers, restaurants or hotels. Please let us know of any misuses: lonelyplanet.com/ip.